Franklin B. Hough

The northern Invasion of October 1780

Franklin B. Hough

The northern Invasion of October 1780

ISBN/EAN: 9783337148805

Printed in Europe, USA, Canada, Australia, Japan

Cover: Foto ©ninafisch / pixelio.de

More available books at **www.hansebooks.com**

THE

NORTHERN INVASION

OF

OCTOBER 1780

A SERIES OF PAPERS RELATING TO THE EXPEDITIONS FROM
CANADA UNDER SIR JOHN JOHNSON AND OTHERS

AGAINST

The Frontiers of New York

WHICH WERE SUPPOSED TO HAVE

CONNECTION WITH ARNOLD'S TREASON

PREPARED FROM THE ORIGINALS

WITH AN INTRODUCTION AND NOTES

BY

FRANKLIN B. HOUGH

NEW YORK
M DCCC LXVI

SUBSCRIBER'S COPY.

No.

PUBLICATIONS

OF THE

BRADFORD CLUB.

No. I.—Papers concerning the Attack on
        Hatfield and Deerfield .   1859
"   II.—The Croakers   1860
"   III.—The Operations of the French Fleet
         under Count De Grasse   1864
"   IV.—Anthology of New Netherland   1865
     V.—Narratives of the Career of
         De Soto in Florida .   1866
"   VI.—Northern Invasion   1866

EXTRA NUMBER.

Memorial of John Allan   -   1864

THE BRADFORD CLUB.

UNDER this designation, a few gentlemen, interested in the study of American History and Literature, propose occasionally to print limited editions of such manuscripts and scarce pamphlets as may be deemed of value towards illustrating these subjects. They will seek to obtain for this purpose unpublished journals or correspondence containing matter worthy of record, and which may not properly be included in the Historical Collections or Documentary Histories of the several States. Such unpretending contemporary chronicles often throw precious light upon the motives of action and the imperfectly narrated events of bygone days; perhaps briefly touched upon in dry official documents.

The Club may also issue fac-similes of curious manuscripts, or documents worthy of notice, which, like the printed issues, will bear its imprint.

" These are the
Registers, the chronicles of the age
They were written in, and speak the truth of History
Better than a hundred of your printed
Communications." — *Shakerly Marmyon's Antiquary.*

WILLIAM BRADFORD — the first New York Printer — whose name the Club has adopted, came to this country in 1682,

and established his Press in the neighborhood of Philadelphia.
In 1693 he removed to this City — was appointed Royal
Printer — and set up his Press "at the Sign of the Bible."
For upwards of thirty years he was the only Printer in the
Province, and in 1725 published our first Newspaper — *The
New York Gazette*. He conducted this paper until 1743 when
he retired from business. He died in May, 1752, and was
described, in an obituary notice of the day, as "a man of great
sobriety and industry, a real friend to the poor and needy, and
kind and affable to all." He was buried in Trinity Church
Yard, by the side of the wife of his youth; and the loving
affection of relatives and friends reared a simple and unostentatious Monument to his memory.

CONTENTS.

	PAGE.
Introduction,	17
Letter from Colonel Bellinger, Sept. 1, 1780,	65
Letter from Colonel Van Schaick to Governor Clinton, Sept. 6, 1780,	67
Letter from Lieutenant Colonel Jansen to Governor Clinton, Sept. 18, 1780,	69
Letter from Governor Clinton to Lieutenant Colonel Jansen, Sept. 18, 1780,	69
Letter from Governor Clinton to Lieutenant Colonel Newkirk, Sept. 18, 1780,	70
Letter from Lieutenant Colonel Jansen to Governor Clinton, Sept. 19, 1780,	71
Letter from Governor Clinton to Colonel Pawling, Sept. 21, 1780,	72
Letter from Colonel J. Newkirk to Governor Clinton, Sept. 23, 1780,	73
Letter from Governor Clinton to General Washington, Sept. 1, 1780,	74
Letter from General Robert Van Rensselaer to Governor Clinton, Sept. 4, 1780,	76
Letter from Colonel Patterson and others, to Governor Clinton, Sept. 11, 1780,	77
Letter from Governor Clinton to persons in Cumberland county, Sept. 16, 1780,	78
Letter from Colonel G. Van Schaick to Governor Clinton, Sept. 12, 1780,	79
Letter from Governor Clinton to Colonel G. Van Schaick, Sept. 14, 1780,	81

CONTENTS.

	PAGE.
Extract from *Rivington's Royal Gazette*, Sept. 23, 1780,	81
Letter from Governor Clinton to General Schuyler, Oct. 3, 1780,	82
Letter from citizens of Tryon county to Governor Clinton, Oct. 3, 1780,	83
Petition from citizens of Tryon county, Oct. 6, 1780,	85
Letter from Governor Clinton to Colonel Klock, Oct. 11, 1780,	87
Letter from Stephen Lush to Governor Clinton, Oct. 12, 1780,	89
Articles of capitulation of Fort George,	92
Letter from Colonel W. Malcom to General Van Rensselaer, Oct. 13, 1780,	93
Letter from General Van Rensselaer to Governor Clinton, Oct. 13, 1780,	94
Reply of Governor Clinton to General Van Rensselaer, Oct. 14, 1780,	95
Account of the attack upon Forts Ann and George, from Holt's Journal, Oct. 16, 1780,	95
Letter from Governor Clinton to General Greene, Oct. 14, 1780,	96
Letter from Governor Clinton to General Washington, Oct. 14, 1780,	97
Letter from Captain Sherwood to Colonel Henry Livingston, Oct. 17, 1780,	99
Letter from General Heath to Governor Clinton, Oct. 17, 1780,	101
Letter from Lieutenant Colonel Veeder to Henry Glen, Oct. 17, 1780,	102
Letter from General Robert Van Rensselaer to Governor Clinton, Oct. 18, 1780,	103
Letter from Governor Clinton to General Schuyler, Oct. 18, 1780,	105
Letter from Lieutenant Colonel Barent I. Staats to Governor Clinton, Oct. 18, 1780,	106
Letter from Major J. Lansing to Governor Clinton, Oct. 18, 1780,	107
Letter from Governor Clinton to General Washington, Oct. 18, 1780,	108
Letter from Governor Chittenden of Vermont to Governor Clinton, Oct. 18, 1780,	111
Letter from Isaac Stoutenburgh to Governor Clinton, Oct. 19, 1780,	112

CONTENTS.

	PAGE.
Letter from General Ten Broeck to Governor Clinton, Oct. 19, 1780,	113
Letter from General Ten Broeck to Governor Clinton, Oct. 19, [1780],	114
Letter from General Van Rensselaer to Governor Clinton, [Oct. 19, 1780],	115
Letter from Sampson Dyckman to Governor Clinton, [Oct. 19, 1780],	117
Letter from General Robert Van Rensselaer to Governor Clinton, [Oct. 19, 1780],	117
Letter from Colonel Lewis Dubois to General Van Rensselaer, [Oct. 20, 1780],	118
Letter from Colonel Lewis Dubois to Governor Clinton, [Oct. 20, 1780],	119
Warrant for impressing cattle and flour,	120
A return of ordnance and stores taken from the British Army commanded by Sir John Johnson, Oct. 19, 1780,	121
Notice of Northern Invasion from Loudon's Paper, Oct. 19, 1780,	121
Letter from General Schuyler to Governor Clinton, Oct. 20, 1780,	123
Letter from Governor Clinton to General Schuyler, Oct. 26, 1780,	125
Letter from Governor Clinton to Colonel Klock, Oct. 23, 1780,	126
Letter from Governor Clinton to Colonel Bellinger, Oct. 23, 1780,	126
Order for garrisoning Frontier Posts, Oct. 23, 1780,	127
Letter from Colonel Alexander Webster to Governor Clinton, Oct. 24, 1780,	128
Extract of a letter from Captain Jonathan Lawrence, Junior, to Colonel Samuel Drake, Oct. 24, 1780,	129
Memorial from the Inhabitants of Schenectady, Oct. 24, 1780,	131
Letter from Governor Clinton to Ebenezer Russell, Oct. 26, 1780,	132
Letter from Governor Haldimand of Canada, with lists of casualties, Oct. 25, 1780,	133
Address of the Mayor and Common Council of Albany to Governor Clinton, Oct. 26, 1780,	137
Reply of Governor Clinton to the foregoing address,	139
Marching orders of Colonel Weissenfels, Oct. 26, 1780,	140
Letter from General Schuyler to Governor Clinton, Oct. 27, 1780,	140

xii   CONTENTS.

                                                                    PAGE.
Letter from General Ten Broeck to Governor Clinton, Oct. 29,
   1780,..   142
Letter from Colonel Lewis Van Woert to General Ten Broeck,
   Oct. 28, 1780,..   142
Letter from Governor Clinton to James Duane, Oct. 29, 1780,.   143
Letter from Governor Clinton to General Heath, Oct. 30, 1780, 147
Letter from General Ten Broeck to Governor Clinton, Oct. 30,
   1780,..   150
Letter from Governor Clinton to General Washington, Oct. 30,
   1780,..   151
Letter from Governor Clinton to General Washington, Oct. 31,
   1780,..   157
Letter from General Washington to Governor Clinton, November [5], 1780, ...   159
Proceedings of a Court of Inquiry upon the conduct of General
   Robert Van Rensselaer, March, 1781,....................   164
Memorial of the Supervisors of Tryon County,..............   209
Tabular Summary of Casualties in Tryon County,............   215
Index, ...   217

PREFACE.

Few regions have presented more frequent or more tragic examples of the horrors of war than did the Mohawk valley during the American Revolution. The settlements extending in a narrow strip up into the wilderness, more than fifty miles beyond the general outline of the frontiers, were exposed on every side and at all times to an attack of the enemy, who, favored by long lines of water communication, could approach from the north, west or south, strike at the most exposed points, and retire before pursuit could be made.

If we bear in mind that the hostile parties who infested this region were often made up of those who had been former inhabitants of the valley, or at least were always led by those who had been forced from their homes by the events of the war, and were inflamed with the fiercest revenge against their former neighbors, whom they often found enjoying the property from which they had been driven, we may well infer that this partizan warfare would be active, unrelenting and cruel.

The events of this period upon the western frontiers of New York could never be forgotten by the survivors or their descendants, and most of the traditions gathered from the aged witnesses, or received at second hand from their accounts, have passed into written narratives, and claim credit as history. Although founded upon facts, and in the main correct, as to time, place and circumstances, many of these narratives are warped by prejudice or inflamed by passion, and none of them can claim the merit of presenting the motives which actuated those who controlled the military movements of the occasion, the information upon which they acted, or the difficulties they had to overcome.

The sufferers from an incursion of the enemy could see that no relief came, although timely application had been made; but they could not know the reasons that prevented. They knew that the enemy had escaped with impunity, and might very bitterly complain of the result, which, under all the circumstances, absolutely could not be prevented.

This reflection has often occurred to the editor of this volume in looking through the public records of the revolution. But, perhaps, in none of these are the generally received accounts, and the inferences derived therefrom, more widely different from truth than those relating to the invasions from Canada in the autumn of 1780, in which the enemy's main body, under Sir John Johnson, after sweeping through the Schoharie and Mohawk valleys, destroying every thing left by former invasions and not guarded by force, eluded pursuit, and returned with comparatively small loss to Canada. The official documents relating to this invasion were found so full and ample, that it was thought advisable to collect and preserve them together, to the end that history might stand corrected, so far as it related to these events, although at variance with every statement hitherto published concerning them.

In arranging these papers, attention has been paid to connection of subjects rather than to strict order of time, and the documents have been used without abridgment, although sometimes relating to subjects not connected with the principal events in view. It was not deemed necessary to extend the series by including the papers relating to exchange of prisoners, and other subjects incidentally resulting from the invasion described; but it is believed enough will be found to justify the conclusion that no charge of inefficiency, cowardice or intentional wrong can be properly laid against those acting under the authority of the state upon that occasion.

"THIS ENTERPRISE OF THE ENEMY, IS PROBABLY THE EFFECT OF ARNOLD'S TREASON."

Gov. Clinton to Gen. Washington, Oct. 17, 1780.

"IT IS THOUGHT, AND PERHAPS NOT WITHOUT FOUNDATION, THAT THIS INCURSION WAS MADE, UPON THE SUPPOSITION THAT ARNOLD'S TREACHERY HAD SUCCEEDED."

Washington to President of Congress. Oct. 21, 1780.

INTRODUCTION.

The invasion of the Indian settlements upon the Genesee by General Sullivan, in the autumn of 1779, occasioned great distress among the natives, who were driven to seek shelter at Fort Niagara. The destruction had been sweeping, and the miseries which followed, during the hard winter of 1779-80 were severe; but although crops and settlements were laid waste, most of the Indian warriors escaped, and very naturally soon began to meditate plans of revenge. The villages of the Oneida tribe friendly to the Americans, were menaced during the winter, and while the snow yet lay deep in the forests, and the streams were bridged with ice, the war parties of Brant and Butler began active hostilities, along the whole northern and western frontiers of New York. These incursions, although not accompanied by scenes of butchery, like those perpetrated at Wyoming and Cherry Valley, were still marked with incidents of thrilling terror, and were attended with great loss of property; many prisoners were led into captivity, many lives were sacrificed, and the greatest alarm was spread throughout the border counties.

The first of their hostile parties appeared on the 15th of March, 1780, at Reimensnyder's Bush, four miles north of the Little Falls, where they took Captain John Keyser, his two sons and two other prisoners, killed one man, burned the captain's house, killed his stock, and left his wife and babes destitute. A body of militia was called out, but from want of snow shoes could not pursue. The party was reported about fifty in number, chiefly tories disguised as Indians, and from their tracks they appeared to have come from the country of the Five Nations. It was strongly suspected, that some unfriendly Oneidas had been privy to this movement, and had harbored the party.[1]

Six days later, about one hundred Indians from Canada, with three tories from Ballston and Tryon, surprised a small post at Skeenesborough, captured its little garrison of thirteen men, killed and scalped a man and his wife, burnt several buildings, and retired down the lake on the ice, by the way they came.[2]

On the 3d of April, a party of tories and Indians said to be sixty in number returned to Reimensnyder's Bush, burnt a mill, and carried off nineteen prisoners from that settlement northward into Canada. On the same day, a block-house on the Sacondaga, north of

---
[1] *Clinton Papers*, No. 2,751.
[2] Letter of Gen. Abraham Ten Broeck.—*Clinton Papers* Nos. 2,758, 2,767.

Johnstown, was attacked by a party of seven Indians, who attempted to set it on fire, but were prevented by the activity and boldness of one man, its sole occupant,[1] who extinguished the fire and severely wounded one of the number. When they had retired, he rallied six others, pursued and killed the whole of the invading party.

On the 7th of April, Brant with a small party of tories and Indians, on their way to surprise Schoharie, came upon a few men under Capt. Alexander Harper, engaged in making maple sugar at Harpersfield. Three of the number were killed, and eleven or twelve taken prisoners to Niagara.[2] It is said that Brant was dissuaded from his first design of striking at Schoharie, by the fictitious declarations of Captain Harper, that large reinforcements had arrived at that place. On this expedition, Brant detached a small party which fell upon the Minisink settlement, and brought off several prisoners.

Simultaneous with these events, intelligence was brought to the commander-in-chief, of preparations by the enemy, in the collection of munitions, horses, vessels and boats, which seemed to indicate an intention of operating in force against the American posts on the Hudson.

These events occurring at so early a period, seemed to

---

[1] Solomon Woodward.

[2] *Campbell's Tryon County*, 1st ed., 159 : *Stone's Life of Brant*, ii, 56 : *Simms's Schoharie County*, 325. Captain Harper remained a captive till November 28, 1782.

indicate a troublesome and dangerous summer on the frontiers. The minds of the inhabitants were filled with the most gloomy apprehensions, and Colonel Yates in writing from Palatine upon the Mohawk, intimated, that unless a number of troops sufficient to protect the settlements could be sent up, very few of the inhabitants in that section would remain.

"The country," said he, "is very extensive, and lies open on all sides to the inroads of the savages. I need not describe to you the distresses of such as are obliged to abandon their habitations, and the consequent distress and inconvenience of such as they fly to for refuge, besides the preventing of which, the crops now in the ground, and those to be put in, must (I should rather say ought to) be saved, or there will be famine to those who are now residing here. I have every opportunity to convince myself, that people have bread for no longer than the ensuing harvest. Indeed too many have not that."[1]

These inroads upon the frontiers, called for active measures for the public safety. Guards were stationed at various points on the upper Mohawk, and the militia were ordered to keep themselves in readiness to march at a minute's warning, upon a given signal.

---

[1] *Clinton Papers*, No. 2,751. Col. Christopher P. Yates, the writer of the above, was a leading patriot of Tryon county, and chairman of the committee of correspondence at the beginning of the war. He served as a captain and afterward as a colonel of militia, and was the first county clerk under state appointment. He represented Montgomery county in assembly five years, and died on his farm three miles west of Canajoharie, and a mile from the river, Jan. 21, 1814, at the age of 65 years.

INTRODUCTION.

Before further tracing the events of 1780, we will briefly describe the extent of the settlements in Albany and Tryon counties, and the defenses then existing for their protection.

The Mohawk valley, at the beginning of the revolution, had a population of about ten thousand, scattered along in a narrow belt as far west as the present town of German Flatts, in Herkimer county. Northward, the settlements extended to a short distance beyond Johnstown. Towards the south, they had reached the head waters of the Susquehanna, and in the valley of the Schoharie creek, to about seven miles beyond Middleburgh. Northward of Albany, they were thinly scattered over the southern and eastern portions of the present county of Saratoga, and in Washington (then Charlotte) county, to Skeenesborough, now Whitehall. Small settlements had been commenced on the western shores of Lake Champlain, and considerable, yet widely scattered improvements had been made in Cumberland county, then claimed by New York, but now included in Vermont. At the beginning of hostilities, many of the inhabitants decided to support the royal cause, especially among the Scotch settlers near Johnstown, although loyalists were found in almost every district in the colony.

Their relative number was not large, but their families often remained in the country, a burden upon society, and objects of constant suspicion and jealousy with those friendly to the American cause. They harbored the enemies' spies, procured information, and secretly favored his movements as opportunities offered. Those who had fled to the enemy to bear arms for the king, proved the most dangerous and vindictive of partizans, being thoroughly acquainted with the topography of the country, and familiar with every road and stream and valley, that would favor the movements of an invading party, or of a lurking foe.

The invasion of General Burgoyne, from the north, and repeated inroads upon the Mohawk frontiers, had entirely broken up the feeble beginnings upon Lake Champlain, and the thriving settlements of Cherry Valley, Newtown-Martin, Springfield, Harpersfield, and Andrustown, southward of the Mohawk. Over six hundred persons from Tryon county alone, had gone off to the enemy, and hundreds of farms all around the borders of civilization, were abandoned by their owners, or destroyed by the enemy, leaving dreary solitudes in places that had lately been enlivened by industry, and with here and there a heap of rubbish to mark the site of what had been a home.

During the French and Indian wars, fortifications had been erected at various points along the frontiers, and the troubles of the revolution led to the construction of stockades around dwellings at numerous places throughout the country, for sheltering of the inhabitants in times of danger.

The number of these outposts having led to a greater distribution of the troops available for their defense

INTRODUCTION. 23

than was thought desirable, the board of war, about the middle of March, decided to break up several minor stations, including those at Schenectady, Schoharie, Johnstown, Fort Plank, Oneida Castle, Half Moon Point, New City, Saratoga, Fort Edward, and Skeenesborough. The events upon the frontiers, already noticed, induced Governor Clinton to retain some of those at Skeenesborough, Fort Plank, Herkimer, Schoharie, and Fort Edward.

Fort Schuyler, on the site of the present village of Rome, was then the most important post on the frontier, and of sufficient strength to resist a large force.[1] During a part of the summer of 1780, it was garrisoned by Colonel Van Schaick of the Continental troops, but early in September, he was ordered to join the grand army, and Major Hughes was left in command. It was the frontier post on the Mohawk, and nearly thirty miles beyond the settlements. Fort Herkimer on the south bank of the Mohawk, opposite the mouth of West Canada creek, and Fort Dayton in the present village of Herkimer, were then garrisoned by small bodies of troops. At the former, a company of fifteen men had been stationed during the winter under Lieutenant John Smith, for the protection of military stores. Their time had expired in April, and they were clamoring for their discharge. Fort Plain,

---

[1] A return of artillery at Fort Schuyler, made November 23, 1780, showed that there were then 22 cannon and 6 mortars, mostly iron pieces and mounted for garrison use.

half a mile west of the present village of that name, and Fort Hunter, east of the Schoharie creek, near its confluence with the Mohawk, were works that could oppose a hand attack. In the Schoharie settlements there were three small forts, and on the northern frontier there were forts with feeble garrisons at Lake George, Fort Ann, Skeenesborough, Fort Edward, and a few other points. Some of these were mere blockhouses, others were old works in partial ruin, and none of them of sufficient strength to resist a vigorous assault.

The territorial divisions of Albany and Tryon counties as they existed in 1780, will be understood by reference to the accompanying map.[1]

The militia of that portion of the state not in the power of the enemy, was organized into forty-five regiments, of which seventeen were in Albany, one in Charlotte, one in Cumberland, eight in Dutchess, three in Orange, five in Tryon, four in Ulster, and six in Westchester counties. Of these, two were composed wholly of exempts, and in addition to the regimental organizations above enumerated, there were twenty-five companies of associated exempts, whose officers had received commissions from the state council of appointment. The militia were only called out as occasional alarms or invasions made it necessary, the

---

[1] The colonial act dividing Albany and Tryon counties into districts, was passed March 22d, 1772, and amended March 8, 1773, by changing the names of the districts as given in the map.

duty of guarding the advanced posts, being chiefly entrusted to detachments from the Continental army, and to levies raised from time to time, and usually for but short periods, for the special duty of defending the frontiers.

During the summer of 1779, two distinct corps of five hundred men each, had been ordered by the legislature for this service, and placed under Lieutenant Colonels Albert Pawling and Henry K. Van Rensselaer. To replace these, a law was passed March 11th, 1780, for raising eight hundred men by detachments from the state militia, whenever congress should declare that these troops should be paid and subsisted by the United States. The necessary action was taken by congress on the 4th of April, but the levies were not raised and organized in time to prevent the mischief against which they were intended to guard. Yet there was no needless delay in perfecting these plans, and the correspondence of the period shows, that while the inhabitants along the frontiers were trembling at the premonitions of coming dangers, the executive was making every effort to meet the emergencies of the impending crisis.

The commander-in-chief was at this time embarrassed by the expiration of the period of enlistment of many troops in the Continental army, and the governors of New Jersey and New York were requested to take measures for assembling the militia in case of danger, and to detach a portion for garrison duty until a reörganization could be effected. The letters of commanding officers at this period were burdened with complaints of the scarcity of provisions, which greatly delayed all military movements, and demanded the most active exertions to keep the army supplied.

We will now resume our narrative of events upon the frontiers. On the 29th of April, a prisoner taken at Skeenesborough, escaped from prison at Montreal, and in fifteen days reached home, with intelligence that extensive preparations were being made for an invasion from Canada. Col. Jacob Klock, on the 12th of May, wrote to the governor from Fort Paris, in the Stone Arabia settlement, that he had evidence that convinced him of the approach of Sir John Johnson towards Johnstown, and that Brant with a band of tories and Indians, was expected to fall at the same time upon Canajoharie. These events would have happened before this date, had not the melting snows and spring floods prevented. The disaffected throughout the valley were expecting these movements, and it was rumored that considerable bodies of tories had been enrolled, for the purpose of joining the invaders when they appeared.[1]

---

[1] We have been more minute in stating these facts, to correct an error of the late William L. Stone in his *Life of Brant*. He says, "The first blow was as sudden as it was unexpected, especially from the quarter whence it came. On Sunday the 21st of May, at dead of night, Sir John Johnson entered the north part of Johnstown — * * * ; and so entirely unawares had he stolen upon the sleeping inhabitants, that he arrived in the heart of the country undiscovered except by the resident loyalists who were probably in the secret."—*Life of Brant*, ii, 72.

INTRODUCTION. 27

These rumors threw the country into the greatest alarm, and Col. Van Schaick writing from Albany of the 17th of May, informed the governor that he was receiving hourly applications from the north and west for aid, that the more remote settlements were daily breaking up and moving down the country, and that unless something was speedily done to check the alarm, the whole region west of Schenectady and north of Albany would be abandoned. Under these circumstances one half of General Ten Broeck's brigade was ordered out, to meet the coming invasion. The regiments of Colonels Yates, Van Woert, Schoonhoven and McCrea had assembled at Saratoga on the 20th of May. On the 18th, troops were dispatched from Albany for Stone Arabia, and other reinforcements were hastened forward for the defense of the valley as they could be assembled. Five full regiments were ordered into Tryon county and the Schoharie settlements, but as it was still uncertain where the blow would fall, they were held in reserve until the movements of the enemy could be definitely ascertained.

In the meantime Sir John Johnson with a force reported as consisting of four hundred whites, from his own and Butler's regiments, and the regulars with two hundred Indians, proceeded in vessels up Lake Champlain to Crown Point.[1] Leaving his boats and

---

[1] *Clinton Papers*, No. 2,893.

vessels at the head of Bulwagga bay, under a small guard, he struck into the forest toward the upper Hudson, and from thence following up the Sacondaga valley, he appeared on Sunday night, May 21st, at his former residence near Johnstown. There was at this period a stockade around the court-house, with a garrison sufficient for its defense, but too feeble for hostile movements. Without spending time upon this, he detached a part of his force, to proceed further down the river and strike the Mohawk at or below Tribe's hill. Their route led along familiar roads, and through friendly neighborhoods. The invaders were minutely informed of every circumstance that could favor or impede their movements, and the political bias of every inhabitant was well known; the victims of revenge were selected, and the details of their operations were arranged.

A little before daybreak on Monday morning, the blow fell, and their course up the valley from Tribe's hill to the Nose,[1] was marked by scenes of conflagration, pillage and murder; yet even in this, the hand of the destroyer was somewhat stayed, and no violence was offered to women and children.[2] The houses of tories were spared, and great numbers of loyalists joined the invaders upon their return towards Johns-

[1] A gorge on the Mohawk between the present towns of Palatine and Root.
[2] *Clinton Papers*, No. 2,910. Minute details of this invasion are given in *Stone's Life of Brant*, ii, 72, and in *Simms's Schoharie County*, p. 343.

town. In the meantime, a quantity of plate and treasure which had been buried at the baronial hall by a faithful slave, after its abandonment in 1776, was recovered by Sir John, and having accomplished the main objects of the expedition, he prepared for his return to Canada. Excepting ten or a dozen houses owned by tories, every dwelling on the route of the invaders, on the north bank of the Mohawk, for a distance of over ten miles, had been burned; many prisoners were taken, and numbers of negro slaves were recovered by their former masters.

On the evening of the same day, Sir John retired to Mayfield, where he encamped. On the first day he proceeded seven miles, and on the second fourteen, his course being in the direction of Lake Champlain. A party of militia under Colonels Harper and Vrooman, and a body of troops from Schenectady under Colonel Van Schaick, undertook to pursue him, but want of provisions delayed their movements until they were too late for effect. Governor Clinton hastened from Kingston upon the first alarm, and with such troops as he could rally in Albany and Charlotte counties, marched to Fort George. Ordering Major Allen and Colonel Warner to meet him at Ticonderoga, with such militia as could be rallied on the New Hampshire Grants, he finally, on the eighth day after leaving Kingston, succeeded in crossing Lake George, from whence he hastened to Crown Point; but the retreating enemy were safe beyond pursuit, having embarked six hours before for St. John.[1] The delay in procuring boats and provisions at Lake George had disappointed his efforts, and after taking measures for covering the frontier against further inroad from Canada, he returned.[2]

Public rumor had led to an expectation of an attack from the westward under Brant, but if this had originally been intended, some event had thus far prevented its execution. The protection of the Mohawk settlements was, however, of the utmost importance, and the condition of Fort Schuyler especially called for prompt action on the part of the commander-in-chief. The militia of Tryon county had for a long period been relied upon for garrison duty at this post, and the dangers that hung over their families made these soldiers restive under the restraints of this service, and anxious to be at their homes for their protection. This feeling had increased until it almost amounted to open mutiny, and early in the summer, General Washington ordered Colonel Van Schaick with two hundred and fifty levies to proceed thither. The recent movements of the enemy had appeared to menace his post, and common prudence demanded that it should be secured

---

[1] *Clinton Papers*, 2,972, 2,973. The governor expressed his gratification at the promptness with which the troops from the Grants were raised and marched to his aid.

[2] Anecdotes of this passage down the lakes by Governor Clinton, are given by the author of the *Sexagenary* (edition of 1866, p. 177), but with a mistake in the time, which is there given as following the invasion of October, which forms the principal subject of this volume.

against a surprise, and provisioned against danger from a siege. The militia who were so discontented in garrison, would not be the less reliable for the public defense, and they gladly embraced the opportunity of guarding the minor posts that were scattered through the settlements, and nearer their own homes. Their discontent was in no degree inspired by cowardice, but by a natural, and perhaps pardonable anxiety to be with their families, who were constantly in danger, and frequently driven by real or false alarms to seek refuge in their block-houses. It was manifestly the policy of the enemy to multiply these alarms by their small parties, scattered along the borders of the settlements, and to magnify the fears of the inhabitants. In this they were but too well favored by the presence of the disaffected families in the country, who were willing to give currency to every rumor tending to their interests, whether founded upon facts or fiction.

The larger portion of the Oneidas, and a small part of the Tuscaroras, had hitherto remained friendly to the American cause; but the influence of British agents, and of the other tribes of the Six Nations, was brought strongly to bear upon them, to induce their removal to Niagara. Seonondo, a leading chief, was imprisoned at Niagara, and every argument by way of threat and promise, was used to effect this end. Under this pressure, and to secure that quiet which was denied them in their own settlements, some evinced a willingness to yield; and to prevent such a misfortune about

32   INTRODUCTION.

four hundred of these people were removed to the neighborhood of Schenectady and there supported, at the public cost.¹

The movements of the enemy at New York, and the return of Sir Henry Clinton from his successful enterprise against Charleston, were additional sources of anxiety, and led to repeated and pressing calls for militia to assist in guarding the passes of the Highlands. The state legislature, therefore, on the 24th of June provided for raising a force by drafts from the militia for a period of three months, and General Robert Van Rensselaer, who had recently been promoted from a colonel, to the command of the second brigade of Albany county militia, was ordered to proceed to Stone Arabia and take command at Fort Paris.²

---

¹ In July, 1780, Jellis Fonda was a contractor for supplying 390 rations daily to destitute Oneidas and Tuscaroras at Schenectady. The cinders of their camp fires may still be traced on the brow of the hills southeast of the city.

We find nothing among the *Clinton Papers* to justify the statement of Colonel Stone (*Life of Brant* i, 55), relative to the destruction of the Oneida settlements by the enemy during the winter of 1779-80, and are led to believe, that the removal of these people to a place of safety in the interior was a measure of policy, rather than of actual necessity from the presence of an enemy. Their country might still be justly spoken of as abandoned and laid waste, their industry and prosperity as destroyed, and their condition as in every way injured and impoverished by the war.

² This was a block-house surrounded by a stockade situated on a swell of ground about a half a mile east by north from the churches at Stone Arabia in the town of Palatine. The surface descends from this point northward towards the valley of Garoga creek, and southward to the Mohawk, and it is the most elevated place within several

Early in July large bodies of the enemy were reported as seen near the old Oneida castle; but nothing definite was discovered, nor is their presence there at that time certainly known.

Lurking parties of the enemy were continually prowling along the frontiers, and an occasional fire, or murder, and the sudden disappearance of individuals as prisoners, kept the troops on the alert, and the country in frequent alarm. The cultivation of the fields, except in the vicinity of block-houses, was necessarily abandoned; and the transportation of supplies for the forts was never attempted without a military guard.

On the 26th of July, a large party of the enemy, chiefly Indians, and said to be eight hundred strong, under Brant, with several British officers, appeared before Fort Schuyler, killed several horses and cattle in the adjacent fields, and began a fire of musketry upon the fort, which they continued until nine o'clock in the evening. The news of this event, reaching General Van Rensselaer at Stone Arabia, he immediately set out for the relief of the place, and for the purpose of guarding several bateaux laden with

miles of the locality. The block-house after being removed and used many years as a barn has disappeared, leaving in the open fields only a single aged fruit tree to mark the vicinity of this place of refuge for the surrounding settlements. Fort Paris was named in honor of Isaac Paris, an English emigrant, who settled in Tryon county a few years before the revolution, was naturalized March 20th, 1762, and fell in the battle of Oriskany in August 1777, while serving as colonel of militia.

provisions then on their way up the river. To assist in this service, nearly every able bodied man in the vicinity of Canajoharie was called out. It was currently reported that the fort was about to be invested by a force of British regulars, and it was felt that every exertion must be made for the safety of that important post.[1] Threats were also circulated by the enemy, that the convoys of the boats would be attacked, and the cargoes destroyed.

Meanwhile the savages, having effected this diversion from their real point of attack, made a circuit to the south (at the same time observing without alarming the troops on their way up the river), and came down on the Canajoharie settlements on the 2d of August, stealthily, but with destructive energy.

This place had been the home of Brant before the war, and doubtless many of his followers were like him, refugees from the places they now saw occupied and enjoyed by others. Finding it impossible to recover their lost possessions, they resolved to make their destruction thorough.

Scattering his forces so as to set fire to many houses at the same instant, the chieftain Brant, began a work of desolation with nothing to stay his progress, and in a brief space of time, accomplished his mission and retired. A report, made two weeks after and upon careful inquiry, returned seventeen as killed, two as

---

[1] *Clinton Papers*, No. 3,111.

scalped and then living, forty-one prisoners led into captivity, fifty-two houses and forty-two barns, a church and a grist mill burned, three hundred cattle and horses killed or driven off, and all the wagons and farming implements burned. Every thing was laid waste except the growing crops, and there remained no means of harvesting these. The ruin extended several miles along the south bank of the Mohawk.

A portion of the families found refuge in Fort Plank, which was not attacked. Most of the prisoners taken were women and children, a few of whom were sent back, but the greater portion endured a long and painful captivity.[1]

The smoke of the burning settlement was seen at a distance of four miles, by an armed party in charge of some laden bateaux, and by the inhabitants of Johnstown; but before they could hasten to the relief of the inhabitants the destruction was complete, and its authors on their way to the Susquehannah. A branch of this expedition at about the same time fell upon a settlement on the Norman's Kill, in Albany

---

[1] A list of these prisoners with their ages and remarks, is found in the *Clinton Papers*, No. 3,127. There were 11 boys, 2 old men, 26 girls under 20, and 10 women.

Cornplanter, the celebrated half-breed Seneca chief was in this expedition. Among the prisoners taken was his own father, a white man named O'Bail. Having marched him ten or twelve miles, he made himself known, and allowed him the alternative of joining his fortunes with his red son, or of returning home. He preferred the latter, and was escorted back in safety to the settlements.—*Life of Mary Jemison. Stone's Life of Brant*, ii, 127.

county, and burned twenty houses. General Van Rensselaer having in the meantime delivered his charge at Fort Schuyler, returned. Tidings of the disaster were quickly conveyed to Albany, and General Ten Broeck ordered a large detachment of militia from Albany and Schenectady, to hasten up the valley for the relief of the distressed inhabitants.

On the 5th of August, five hundred troops of the Massachusetts levies were ordered to march for the protection of the Mohawk settlements,[1] and measures were speedily taken for supplying the immediate wants of such families as had escaped captivity with the loss of every thing. The troops as they arrived, were stationed so as to protect them in harvesting their grain, for present subsistence.

A period of comparative tranquility now followed, and the harvest, which was unusually bountiful this season, was secured without further molestation from the enemy. On the first of September, Colonel Malcom's corps was sent by General Washington for the defense of the frontiers, and the relief of the German Flatts and Fort Schuyler, and a part of the militia who had been called out for a short period returned home. Vague rumors of danger were, however, at times circulated through the country, and small parties appeared frequently upon the frontiers, committing

---

[1] The number of Massachusetts troops that were actually sent up the Mohawk Valley, was considerably less than this number. We have not met with any specific statements of their force.

hostilities as circumstances favored, but not always with impunity.

One of the most heroic incidents which the annals of this period record, occurred on the last day of August, about four miles northeast of Fort Dayton. A party consisting of forty-eight Indians and eighteen whites suddenly fell upon a farmer named John Christian Shell, who was laboring with his six sons in a field. The latter succeeded in reaching their house, excepting two little boys eight years old, who were captured. The house was built for defense, and its occupants including the heroic wife made a most resolute resistance, in which without further loss to themselves, they killed eleven and wounded six or seven of the enemy. Their leader, one Donald McDonald, being wounded at the door, was dragged in by the family, and their house thus secured against being burned by the assailants. The unequal contest continued several hours, when the enemy retired, and the family having provided food for their prisoner withdrew to Fort Dayton, and the next day the wounded who had been left on the premises were brought in.[1] A party was sent in pursuit of the enemy, but returned without success. The two little sons of Mr. Shell returned after a long captivity. He was himself killed the next year by an enemy lurking in ambush.

---

[1] Full details of this event are given in *Benton's Herkimer County*, p. 93, but under an erroneous date. A version in rhyme is found in *Campbell's Tryon County* (1831), p. 71.

The difficulties attending the maintenance of the army, were at this period greatly enhanced by the depreciation of the paper currency that had been issued by congress, and which had fallen since the autumn of 1777, from par to two and a half per cent. This rendered it necessary for the states to levy taxes in kind, for whatever articles were of greatest necessity for the troops. The governor of New York was authorized to issue press warrants for taking cattle, flour, grain, teams and labor, as the emergencies of the service required; and this harsh expedient was employed many times during the summer, when prompt action could not otherwise be secured. The destitution of the army, which at this time formed a most serious obstacle in its operations, was not so much due to absolute want of supplies in the country, as to difficulties attending their collection and transportation.

The maintenance of a garrison at Fort Schuyler, was regarded as essential to the protection of the Mohawk frontier; and the only practicable route for transportation being the Mohawk river, it was highly important that the winter supplies should be forwarded before the river was closed by ice. The boats used in this service always required a convoy, and the navigation, interrupted by frequent rapids and a portage, was attended with great labor.

The conduct of some of the public leaders in Cumberland county was at this period in the highest degree embarrassing to Governor Clinton, and led to serious suspicions of treachery in the mind of General Washington. The party who were endeavoring to establish an independent state government, in defiance of the authority of New York, appeared to be in communication with the enemy, for purposes which could not be ascertained, and under circumstances which led to the worst conjectures as to their motives and designs. The conduct of Colonel Ethan Allen was especially censured, and so far did these suspicions of treachery gain credit, that the commander-in-chief issued orders to General Schuyler, then at Saratoga, to arrest *a certain person*, in the event of certain contingencies, which however did not occur.

These determined advocates of a new state organization declared themselves ready for any alliance that would favor their end, and under the pretext of negotiating for the release of prisoners, engaged in a correspondence which has scarcely been justified by any apology of their friends. Occurring at this juncture, when harmony and confidence were of the greatest importance, it proved a source of anxiety and embarrassment injurious to the public welfare, and encouraging to the enemy. Yet in anticipation of coming favors, the enemy spared the inhabitants of the " Grants " many of the evils they might have easily inflicted, and which were felt with increased severity by the unhappy citizens of northern New York.

During the early part of the autumn of 1780, the return of a scout, or of a prisoner escaped from the enemy, brought intelligence from time to time, of some hostile design in preparation in Canada; but these rumors were vague and disconnected, and nothing transpired to indicate any particular point of danger. These rumors might be merely founded upon some device intended to mislead the military authorities, and distress the inhabitants with constant alarms, and nothing positive could be ascertained relative to the intentions of the enemy. Hostile parties appearing at widely distant points, and occasionally a murder, the disappearance of a person as a prisoner, or the burning of a house, kept the troops at the various stations on the alert, and rendered the designs of the enemy more difficult to determine.

One of these parties appeared at Shawangunk on the 18th of September, attacked the house of Colonel Johannis Jansen, killed and scalped two young women and an old man, and carried away three negro slaves. Two regiments of militia were ordered in pursuit, but found no trace of the assailants, who were believed to be tories, and former residents of the district.

The earlier invasions of this season, and public business depending in congress upon the action of New York, made it necessary to call an extra session of the legislature, which met in Poughkeepsie on the 7th of September. In his opening message, the governor stated the insufficiency of the force on the frontiers, for their adequate defense, the embarrass-

INTRODUCTION.

ments attending enlistments in the Continental service, the destitution of the army, and the necessity of granting more power to congress. The Articles of Confederation then under consideration had not yet been ratified, and the general congress had hitherto been able only to recommend to the several states, such measures as it should itself have had the power to enforce. This session of the legislature ended on the 10th of October, and was chiefly occupied in considering the military necessities of the day. It levied taxes upon the several counties payable in cattle and grain, extended former laws authorizing the impress of articles needed in the service, provided for completing the state quota in the Continental army, and gave to the governor all needed powers for the full control of the militia.

Under this law, passed September 29th, the governor could order into the service from time to time as he might deem necessary, such numbers of the militia as might be required for the defense of the frontiers. The men were to be drawn by classes, were to be held for forty-five days from the time of their assembling, and in matters relating to discipline, pay and rations, were placed on a par with the Continental troops. The act embraced the necessary regulations for enforcing the call by fines and forfeitures, for the commutation of quakers, and other details necessary for its successful operation.

In view of the exposed condition of northern New

York, and the importance of protecting the supplies of that region, upon which the troops mainly relied for subsistence during the coming winter; but before any further hostilities were known to be in actual preparation, Brigadier General James Clinton was assigned by General Washington to the command at Albany, and he was authorized by his brother the governor to call upon Generals Ten Broeck and Van Rensselaer for such assistance as their brigades might be able to render in case of need.

On the 1st of October, General Schuyler informed the governor by letter, of certain indications of an approaching invasion by way of Lake Champlain, and on the 6th, a number of citizens of Tryon county united in a petition for immediate assistance, to prepare against an attack from the westward. From intelligence which had been received, it appeared quite certain, that a large force of the enemy under Sir John Johnson, Butler and Brant, had six days before left Niagara, and were then on their way to Oneida. On the 10th, an Indian deserter arrived at Fort Schuyler with news that the enemy were approaching in considerable force, with the view of attacking Stone Arabia, and ultimately Fort Schuyler. He stated that they were furnished with mortars and cannon, with shells in large quantities; and to confirm his statement he exhibited a five inch shell which he had brought with him in his blanket.

Major Hughes in command at that post, immediately

communicated this intelligence; the several garrisons throughout the valley were placed on their guard against a surprise, and detachments of militia were called out.

The force reported as approaching by way of Lake Champlain, consisted of about a thousand men, regulars, loyalists and Indians under Major Christopher Carleton, of the 29th regiment. He came up the lake from St. John's with a fleet of eight vessels and twenty-six boats, and having landed in South Bay, suddenly appeared before Fort Ann on the 10th of October, and demanded its surrender. The garrison consisted of seventy-five men, officers included, under the command of Adiel Sherwood, captain of one of the regiments of levies raised the summer previous to reinforce the Continental army. He had but a scanty supply of ammunition, and being unwilling to exasperate the enemy by using what little he had, after a short consultation among the officers, he surrendered himself and men prisoners of war, reserving only the liberty of sending the women and children to their respective homes.[1] This fort, which was only a block-house rudely built of logs and enclosed by a stockade, was burned, and marauding parties were sent out, who burnt and destroyed portions of the settlements of Kingsbury,

---

[1] Captain Sherwood had previously been a lieutenant in the 1st Continental battalion, but resigned May 16, 1780, and on the 18th of July was appointed to the command above stated. In a letter written by him while a prisoner, he says that the force appearing before him at Fort Ann, consisted of 778 men, chiefly British regulars.

Queensbury and Fort Edward.¹ The smoke of these burnings and the reports of refugees driven in by the enemy, gave information at Fort Edward of the ravages that were being committed above; but Colonel Livingston was not in force to march, and no relief was to be had nearer than from the Albany militia.²

Major Carleton appeared before Fort George on the 11th, but not without some loss by the fire of the garrison. This post was commanded by Captain John Chipman, of the second Continental battalion, and his troops about forty in number, were chiefly composed of drafts from the militia classes, from the neighboring towns of Charlotte county. He was not in condition for vigorous resistance, or a protracted siege; and no relief being in prospect he surrendered upon terms similar to those that had been granted at Fort Ann. The prisoners were transferred to the vessels on Lake Champlain, and the fort was destroyed. Ensign Barrett was permitted to return with his family and the regimental books, upon giving his parole, and two wagons were allowed for the women and children and their effects.³

---

¹ Petition for exemption from taxes in Charlotte county, Jan. 23, 1781, *Legislative Papers*, No. 2,422.

² Fort Edward was temporarily abandoned upon this occasion, but the enemy appeared not to know it, and made no attempt to occupy or destroy it.

³ A deserter named Van Deusen reported a horrid case of torture inflicted upon a soldier in revenge for the death of an Indian; but the charge was repelled in a subsequent correspondence with Colonel Gansevoort. The letters exchanged upon this and other subjects, are given in *Stone's Life of Brant*, ii, 129.

INTRODUCTION.   45

A branch of this expedition, consisting of about four hundred regulars, tories and Indians, under the command of Major John Munro, a tory, formerly a merchant at Schenectady, having left their boats at the head of Bulwagga bay near Crown Point, proceeded by an interior route west of Lake George, with the original intention, as is believed, of surprising Schenectady. Whatever may have been the intended point of attack, the information obtained by their scouts, or other reasons, decided them to proceed no further than the Ballston settlement.

There was at this time a "fort" of oak logs surrounded by a stockade and provided with loop holes for musketry. It stood at the southwest corner of the square, at Academy hill, and had been garrisoned five days before by a small party of Schenectady militia. The enemy decided not to spend time in attacking this, but found a convenient opportunity for surprising several families in their houses, and of executing their destructive mission upon the devoted settlement.

The first attack was made under the guidance of one McDonald, a tory refugee from this neighborhood, upon the house of Mr. James Gordon,[1] a worthy and

---

[1] General Gordon was at this period a member of assembly, in which office he served nine years. From 1791 to 1795 he was in congress, and from 1797 to 1804, he was state senator. He died at Ballston, January 17, 1810. A brief notice of this revolutionary patriot, is found in the *Albany Gazette*, January 19, 1810. We are indebted to the Hon. George G. Scott of Ballston, for most of the above details.

influential citizen, whose strong adherence to the Continental cause, had made him particularly obnoxious to the tories. As his clock was striking the midnight hour on the night of October 16th, he was awakened by the crash of windows broken in with bayonets, and in a brief space of time he and several persons in his employment were secured, and his house pillaged by the Indians. Having killed one man, wounded another as they supposed mortally, and captured twenty-two prisoners in the settlement, they set out to return; but lingered for some time in the northwest corner of the town. They then retired along an Indian trail which led up the Hudson, and along the route by which they came. Fearing an attack, Major Munro issued an order for the prisoners to be instantly killed in case there was the least prospect of their being rescued. For this atrocious order, he was disgracefully dismissed from the service upon his return to Canada. From their first night's encampment, three of the wounded prisoners were allowed to return, and they narrowly escaped an ambuscade that had been laid for the enemy. The party were eight days in returning to their boats, from whence they continued to Montreal. Mr. Gordon was held nearly two years as a prisoner in Canada.

A party consisting of about two hundred, chiefly Indians, under Major Haughton, of the 53d, had set out about the same time from Canada, to fall upon the upper settlements of the Connecticut valley. They succeeded in burning several houses, and in carrying thirty-two inhabitants into captivity.

In the mean time, the enemy who had been reported as in force at Oneida Lake, crossed over to the valley of the Susquehanna. They here probably received reinforcements from Niagara by way of the Tioga route, and proceeded up the eastern branch in the direction of Schoharie, with the view of surprising the posts, and destroying the settlements of that valley. This force, under the command of Sir John Johnson, was composed of regulars, tories and Indians, and was reported to be from eight hundred to a thousand strong.[1] Sir John was accompanied by Colonel Butler and Captain Brant, and many of his men were intimately acquainted with the topography of the country through which they were to pass, having formerly resided in the valley.

We have already noticed that the Schoharie settlements were at this period protected by three forts. The upper fort, completed in 1778,[2] was a one story dwelling owned by John Feeck, enclosed by a stockade, and a breast work. It stood near the upper part of the neighborhood known as Vrooman's land, about five miles west of south from Middleburgh.

---

[1] The enemy's force under Sir John Johnson was reported by Governor Clinton, in writing to General Washington about a fortnight after, to consist of 750 picked troops from the 20th and 34th British regiments, Hessian yagers, Sir John's corps, Butler's rangers, and Brant's corps of Indians and tories.

[2] The land on which this fort stood, is now owned, it is believed, by a descendant of the proprietor in 1780.

48   INTRODUCTION.

The middle fort was at the present village of Middleburgh, from which the latter derived its name. It stood about half a mile east of north from the bridge, and was built around a two story stone house then owned by John Becker. It was a stockade, enclosing about half an acre within the pickets, with block-houses mounted with small cannon upon two of its angles. From its central position it was usually the headquarters of the commandant of the Schoharie posts, and was at this time garrisoned by about two hundred state troops, under the command of Major Melancton L. Woolsey.[1] This fort was built in 1777, and like the former, every vestige has long since disappeared, excepting a small part of the original building.

The lower fort, finished in 1778, had also a stockade

[1] This officer was appointed major in a regiment of levies for the defense of the frontiers, on the 1st of July, 1780, and subsequently became a brigadier general of militia. By an unfortunate turn in trade he became involved, and in 1785, was a petitioner for relief by an act of insolvency. On the 7th of March he was appointed county clerk of Clinton county upon its organization, and he continued to hold this office twenty years. After a long residence in Plattsburgh, he removed to Trenton in Oneida county, where he died June 29, 1819, in his sixty-third year. He was the father of the late Commodore Melancton T. Woolsey of the navy. The confidence with which Major Woolsey continued to be held by Governor Clinton, and the appointments he received at his hand, sufficiently discredit the traditional stories that have been published concerning his alleged deportment upon the occasion of Sir John Johnson's attack upon the middle fort at Schoharie. These statements were evidently not reported, or if told were not believed, at that period.

Major Woolsey's weekly return of the Schoharie forts, dated September 27, 1780, gave a total of 225, under Captains Lansing, Muller, Foord, Poole and Bogart.

with two block-houses mounted with small cannon. It enclosed a stone church, still standing a mile north of Schoharie Court-house,[1] and also enclosed an area of about half an acre. Along the west side of the enclosure were small huts built of rough boards, for the accommodation of families, and for the shelter of their most valuable effects. It was about six miles down the valley, north of the middle fort,[2] and was at this period commanded by Lieutenant Colonel Volkert Veeder.[3]

The approach of the enemy had been conducted with as much secrecy as possible, but two Oneidas having deserted, brought in the intelligence of their movements. It had been expected that the first attack would be made upon the upper fort.

Early in the morning on the 17th of October, the enemy were discovered passing at some distance from the upper fort. A signal gun was fired to notify the posts below of this movement, and their garrisons hastened to make such preparations for defense as their situation allowed. No attempt was made by the enemy to molest the upper fort; but finding themselves discovered, and secrecy no longer possible, they began at once their work of devastation, by setting fire to

---

[1] This building is now owned by the state, and is used as an armory.
[2] *Simms's History of Schoharie County*, p. 269-271.
[3] This officer was commissioned as lieutenant colonel, April 4, 1778, and resigned March 12, 1781. He was six years a member of assembly, and subsequently held the rank of brigadier general in the militia. He died February 22, 1813.

buildings, barns and stacks of grain. Most of the inhabitants had removed their families to the forts, and only went out to the harvest fields armed, and in parties of sufficient force to guard against surprise. As it was still early in the morning, none had gone out, and but few individuals remained at their homes. These were chiefly those who secretly sympathised with the loyalists, and their property was for this reason mostly spared by the invaders, but only to await destruction at the hands of their indignant neighbors, after the enemy were gone.

It was a cold autumnal day, and the driving northwest wind, often laden with sleet, served to fan and spread the fires which the enemy set to the abandoned property of the settlers.

Soon after the first alarm, a party of nineteen volunteers was sent out from the middle fort, to ascertain its cause; but soon returned, having narrowly escaped being surrounded and cut off.[1] The enemy soon appeared before the fort, and some skirmishing ensued between their advanced forces and small parties of the garrison, but without loss on either side.

Colonel Johnson then brought up a small mortar and a brass three pounder field piece, and fired for some

---

[1] *Simms's History of Schoharie County*, p. 402. We have principally followed this author in the above account, omitting many of his details, which were derived entirely from personal recollections and traditions received from the families present upon the occasion. We are not aware of the existence of any official accounts with minute incidents dating at or near the time of these events.

INTRODUCTION.

time upon the fort, but without material effect. An officer and two men were then sent bearing a white flag, but as they approached the fort, they were fired upon.[1] This checked their advance, and they returned. The flag advanced a second and a third time, but was each time stopped by a rifle shot from the fort, when finding further attempt at parley impossible, the firing was resumed. The work of devastation having been completed, and the spirit of the garrison appearing to defy an assault, the invaders about three o'clock in the

---

[1] Popular traditions, and published accounts founded thereon, unite in denouncing Major Woolsey as a coward, and in ascribing the firing upon the flag, to Thomas Murphy, an intrepid partizan of Irish birth, who had formerly belonged to Morgan's Rifle Corps, and had remained at Schoharie after his company were withdrawn. According to these accounts, Major Woolsey was disposed to receive the flag, and to surrender upon any terms that might be offered; but that Murphy, encouraged by the militia officers and the garrison, persisted in stopping it with his rifle, and even threatened violence to the major, should he venture to attempt a negotiation. It is quite probable that the major may have been very unpopular, and the ranger a great favorite with the garrison; but we are not disposed to give credit to the extreme statements respecting either of these persons. The tendency to magnify the faults of an unsuccessful officer, and to multiply anecdotes concerning those who prove themselves energetic and enterprising in times of danger, is too well known to allow us to place dependence upon either, as elements of precise history.

We have a forcible illustration of this, in the traditions that have been embodied in all the histories relating to General Van Rensselaer's pursuit of Sir John Johnson up the Mohawk valley in 1780. Without an exception, these are altogether unfavorable to his reputation. And yet, a court of inquiry, held soon after, and before which all the testimony that enemies could find was produced, failed to detect any fault in his measures, and felt itself constrained to report, " that the whole of his conduct, both before and after, as well as in the action of the 19th of October, was not only unexceptional, but such as become a good, active, faithful, prudent and spirited officer, and

afternoon, desisted from further hostilities, and continued their march down the valley.

But two persons were mortally wounded in the middle fort, while the loss of the enemy is believed to have been greater. The little garrison had expended most of their ammunition when the enemy retired.

Several scouts sent out from the lower fort to learn the progress of events up the valley returned pursued by the enemy, who appeared about four o'clock in the afternoon, and passed this fort upon both sides. Several sharp-shooters were stationed in the tower of the church,

---

that the public clamors raised to his prejudice on that account, are without the least foundation."

We would not, however, in any degree detract from the fame of Timothy Murphy, who well deserved the reputation which his services won him during the troublesome times of the revolution. Intrepid in the face of danger, fond of enterprise, and never quiet, while any thing remained to be done involving perilous adventure, he passed through the war without wound or capture, inspired the enemy with a terror at his name, and earned the gratitude and esteem of the community in which he lived. He owed none of his success to acquired attainments, and although he could neither read nor write, he possessed a native eloquence, which in a rude way had its influence upon the public mind. He passed through life respected as a man of energetic character and upright intentions, and died at his residence near the site of the upper fort, in Middleburgh, Schoharie county, on the 27th of June, 1818. The following epitaph is engraved upon his tomb stone:

"Here too, this warrior sire with honor rests,
Who bared in freedom's cause his valiant breast.
Sprang from his half drawn furrow, as the cry
Of threatened Liberty came thrilling by!
Look'd to his God, and reared in bulwark round,
Breast free from guile, and hands with toil embrowned.
And bade a monarch's thousand banners yield—
Firm at the plough, and glorious in the field.
Lo! here he rests, who every danger braved,
Honored and marked amid the soil he saved."

who were prepared for effective service, and the enemy after firing a few cannon shot, two of which lodged in the timbers of the roof,[1] and burning several buildings in the neighborhood, continued their march without attempting further hostilities at this place, and encamped for the night six miles below.

Intelligence of the presence of the enemy at Schoharie reached Governor Clinton at Albany by noon on the 17th, and Colonel Veeder sent another messenger with a full account of the destruction of the settlements as soon as the enemy had passed the lower fort. Orders were at once sent to General Robert Van Rensselaer, and measures were immediately taken to rally a force of militia sufficient for pursuit. The general arrived at Schenectady towards evening on the 18th, while the horizon towards Schoharie was still glowing with the fires set by the enemy the day before, and lost no time in consulting upon measures for hastening the march of his troops in pursuit of the enemy. He also sent word to Colonel Vrooman, directing him to send such troops as could be spared from the Schoharie forts, to hang upon the rear of the enemy, but to avoid an engagement until he could come up. This order was faithfully executed. His force at that time was about seven hundred men, but more were expected during the night. A few head of cattle intended for Fort Schuyler were slaughtered, and all the ovens in

---

[1] Mr. John Gebhard, jr., of Schoharie, has one of these shot in his possession. The other is owned by Mr. Simms of Fort Plain.

town were put in requisition to supply the troops with bread.

During the evening, General Van Rensselaer called a meeting of the principal citizens, to consult upon means for hastening his march, and it was proposed to use wagons for transporting them a part of the way; but a sufficient number could not be collected during the night, and this plan was abandoned. The troops were bivouacked in the suburbs of the town, and as soon as they could receive their rations in the morning, they began their march up the south side of the river. Governor Clinton, who was then at Albany, took measures for assembling at once such remaining troops and supplies as the country could afford, with the view of following the expedition, and sustaining its movements.

On the morning of the 18th, the enemy resumed their march down the Schoharie valley, and leaving Fort Hunter half a mile to their right, continued up on the south bank of the Mohawk, to a place now known as Willow Basin, a short distance below the Nose, where they encamped for the night. Their route was marked by a general pillage and burning, with the exception of a few houses owned by persons supposed to be of loyal sympathies. Most of the inhabitants were alarmed of the coming danger,[1] in time to escape

---

[1] Some of the dwellings burned upon this occasion were temporary log huts, built to replace the houses destroyed in June by Sir John's troops.

into the fields and woods, where they witnessed the plunder and destruction of their property. A detachment under Captain Duncan,[1] crossed to the north bank, and destroyed what had escaped the invasion of Sir John in May previous, excepting a stone church at Caughnawaga that had been built under the patronage of Sir William Johnson a few years before the war.[2]

On the morning of the 19th, having forded the Mohawk with his main body at Keator's Rift, near the present village of Sprakers, they continued their course up the north side of the valley, as the south, having already been ravaged in August by Brant, had but little left to invite destruction.

General Van Rensselaer continued his march during the day with as much expedition as the state of the roads would admit, and at night on the 18th, had arrived opposite the former residence of Sir William Johnson, about twenty miles above Schenectady. He there halted to rest his troops until the moon arose, and between ten and eleven resumed his march, having in the meantime dispatched a messenger to go around

---

[1] Captain Richard Duncan had formerly lived near Schenectady, and died there in February, 1819. He was for a time member of the executive council of Upper Canada.

[2] This venerable edifice after being used as a church until quite modern times, and afterwards for a short time as an academy, unfortunately became the property of an opulent, but avaricious citizen, who a year or two since, sold the materials for other building purposes. A small part is said to be still left. It stood near the rail road, in the lower part of the village of Fonda. It is to be regretted that the veneration for things ancient, evinced by Sir John's Indians, could not find its counterpart at the present time.

in advance of the enemy, to notify Colonel Brown at Stone Arabia, and Colonel Du Bois at Fort Plain, (then called Fort Rensselaer) of his approach. He ordered them to endeavor to hold the enemy in check until he could come up, when it was hoped that by their combined forces, they might be able to capture the invaders.

Colonel Brown, who then commanded at Fort Paris, in the Stone Arabia settlement, had under him a force of about one hundred and thirty men of the Massachusetts levies, and he was an officer of undoubted ability and tried courage. It is not certainly known whether he received the message of General Van Rensselaer, or whether his movements were occasioned by the rumors he received of the enemy's approach, and his own sense of duty under the circumstances.[1] He, however, formed his command in line of battle, on the morning of the 19th, excepting a few left to guard the fort, and marched down the road leading southward towards the Mohawk. He met the enemy on the slopes of the valley, about a mile from the present village of Palatine Bridge, when a battle ensued that continued to be fought with bravery, until himself and thirty-nine of his men were killed, and two captured. The remainder of his troops broke and fled towards Fort Rensselaer,

---

[1] Governor Clinton states in his correspondence, that Colonel Brown was led by false intelligence into the fire of the whole body of the enemy.

INTRODUCTION.   57

about three miles distant, on the south bank of the river.[1]

The loss of the enemy on this occasion is not known. Forts Keyser and Paris, at Stone Arabia were, at this

---

[1] Colonel Brown was born October 19, 1744, graduated at Yale college in 1771, was educated as a lawyer, married, and settled at Pittsfield in Massachusetts. He took an early interest in the revolution, and accompanied the expedition to Canada in 1776, where he served with much credit, and especially distinguished himself in the capture of Chambly.

During this campaign, Colonel Brown had repeated opportunities for observing the character of Arnold; and judged correctly of the baseness of his principles, and the shallowness of his patriotism. While stationed at Albany the following winter, he publicly and boldly accused the general of treasonable motives, and although these expressions were repeated by Brown in his presence, he did not venture to reply. This hatred to Arnold was cherished to the last, and when the general was arraigned before a court martial, under charges of misconduct while in command at Philadelphia, Colonel Brown sought occasion to tender to the prosecution, the information he possessed concerning his conduct.

In the course of Burgoyne's expedition, Colonel Brown performed an act of successful strategy in the rear of the British army which tended to hasten the result. On the 12th of September, 1777, he was sent by General Lincoln, with five hundred men, to destroy some stores at the north end of Lake George, while another force under Colonel Johnson, was ordered to attack Ticonderoga and Mount Independence. Still another body of militia, under Colonel Woodbridge, was sent forward to Skeenesborough and Fort Ann. Colonel Brown arrived on the heights above the landing on the 17th, attacked the enemy the next morning, and got possession of the landing place, the mills, and a block-house. Captain Ebenezer Allen, with forty Rangers carried Mount Defiance, and the party sent against Ticonderoga surprised and captured a company of troops. These several parties captured 12 officers, 144 British, and 119 Canadians, and 18 artificers, and released 118 American prisoners besides destroying a large quantity of stores.

No mention is made of Colonel Brown in the official reports of these events, as Arnold who then had the ear of Gates, is supposed to have prejudiced that officer against him.

time crowded with families, and capable of but feeble resistance. The enemy had, however, no time to waste in attacking them, and after the defeat of Colonel Brown, they dispersed over a wide extent of

> Tradition relates, that when Colonel Brown formed his men to march out against Sir John Johnson, he was mounted on a black horse, and that after he fell he was scalped. The dead were the next day buried in the grounds adjoining the churches at Stone Arabia, and fifty-six years afterwards, on the anniversary of the battle, a small monument of Berkshire marble was erected at his grave, by his son, the late Henry Brown, Esq., of Berkshire.
>
> This occasion was made impressive by appropriate ceremonies. A large concourse of citizens assembled in the adjoining church. A sermon was preached by the Rev. Abraham Van Horne, and a patriotic address delivered by Mr. Gerrit L. Roof, then a young lawyer at Canajoharie.
>
> In June of the present year (1866), the editor of these pages visited the locality with an artist, to procure a view of the monument, from which the engraving in this volume is made. It stands about three hundred yards west of the Reformed Dutch Church at Stone Arabia, in a large field set apart as a cemetery, but chiefly used as a pasture. The monument is two feet square at the base, by seven in height. Its foundations have settled, giving it an inclination to one side, and a picket fence in ruins, partly encloses it, while a cherry tree of spontaneous growth, overshadows it.
>
> Mr. Roof, who delivered the address in 1836, is now a respected clergyman in Lowville, N. Y. He has kindly furnished us a copy of the following verses written by him, at about the time of that event. They were set to music, and have been favorably noticed.
>
> HE SLEEPS:—THE ICY SEAL OF DEATH.
>
> (Air — *O! bid me not that strain to sing*).
>
>> He sleeps. "The icy seal of death
>> Is set upon his brow."
>> The cannon's roar, he heeds no more,
>> He rests in silence now.
>> The trumpet's clangor's heard afar,
>> And standards proudly wave,
>> But he who braved the battle's shock,
>> Now slumbers in the grave,
>> Now slumbers in the grave.

INTRODUCTION.

country, setting fire to every thing combustible in the settlement.[1]

General Van Rensselaer came up a little before noon, about an hour after the battle was over. He had seen the columns of smoke, and heard the firing;

>He sleeps. The noble warrior sleeps
>Upon the battle plain:
>Nor e'er will he, to victory,
>His comrades lead again.
>His country called him to command,
>He spurned the tyrant's sway;
>The God of battles nerved his arm,
>And glory led the way,
>And glory led the way.
>
>With patriot band he left his home
>To strike for Liberty;
>And march'd to brave the battle's wave,
>Determined to be free.
>His country now his fate deplores,
>His gallant comrades weep:
>He cannot hear their loud laments,
>He sleeps a dreamless sleep,
>He sleeps a dreamless sleep.
>
>Rest Warrior! Thou hast gain'd a wreath
>Of never dying fame;
>And hallow'd be thy memory;
>And honored be thy name.
>Thy spirit, warrior! is with God
>In mansions of the blest,
>The clash of arms, and war's alarms,
>No more disturb thy rest,
>No more disturb thy rest.

[1] Fort Keyser was a stone house stockaded and used as a place of retreat for families in case of alarm from the enemy. It stood on the site of a barn now owned by John A. Failing about a mile and a quarter southeast of Stone Arabia. On the 19th, it was in charge of Captain John Zielie and about half a dozen men. Mr. John Dillenbeck, now (1866) ninety-two years of age, remembers having seen as a child, from an upper window, the flames of some neighbors' houses in the direction of Fort Paris, and a file of red coats passing at some distance to the west. He is probably the only one living, who has any personal recollection of the events of this invasion.

but it was impossible for him to afford timely relief. His force at this time consisted of about nine hundred men, including fifty Oneidas, and after a brief consultation with Colonel Du Bois at Fort Rensselaer, he gave orders for his troops to cross to the north bank as soon as possible. They were exhausted with fatigue, the river was too deep to ford, and the means of crossing were limited to a small ferry, and a rude bridge made by placing wagons in the stream along which the men could climb with difficulty, from one to another. Several hours elapsed before they were all over.

General Van Rensselaer having at length crossed his troops formed them in three columns, the right along the high grounds under Colonel Du Bois, of the levies, the left by Colonel Cuyler of the militia, and the centre by Colonel Whiting, and advanced towards the enemy who were met near Klock's place, about three miles below the present village of St. Johnsville. The enemy formed a line of battle with their rangers on their right, resting upon the river, their regulars in column in the centre, and their Indians and German riflemen on their left about one hundred and fifty yards in advance, in an orchard near Klock's house. The general came up to the enemy about sunset, and an irregular firing began; but his lines soon got into disorder, a portion in front of the rest, and there appeared danger of their firing upon one another. The darkness, which was hastened by the

smoke of burning buildings in the valley, increased
this danger, and after consulting with his officers it
was decided to fall back about a mile and encamp
on the hills. The troops at this time were quite
destitute of supplies; but some were expected during
the night, and it was resolved to renew hostilities early
the next morning.

The enemy were quite as exhausted as their pursuers
by their late march, but with this advantage that they
were abundantly supplied by plundering the country.
Their force and condition did not, however, justify
any further hostilities if they could be avoided, and
during the night they succeeded in crossing again
to the south bank, leaving one small cannon, their
wounded and a part of their plunder in the hands of
their pursuers.

With the first morning light, a party set out to
pursue, and as soon as practicable the whole army was
in motion. But the river was again between them,
and the enemy who had now no time to spare in
plundering and burning made good their retreat by
passing around Fort Herkimer to the south.

The army under General Van Rensselaer reached
Herkimer the next day; but they had lost all trace of
the enemy and the Indian scouts who were sent out
failed to discover their trail. Governor Clinton here
came up and assumed command. Parties were sent
out to within fifteen miles of Oneida; but, although they
found the remains of their last nights' encampment, the

enemy were beyond reach of pursuit, and they returned to Fort Herkimer.

But this brief campaign did not end without still further disaster to the American arms. Major Hughes, commanding at Fort Schuyler, having learned of the place where the enemy had concealed their boats, dispatched a party of men under Captain Vrooman to destroy them, and thus prevent their escape. One of the party having been taken sick, or feigning himself so, was left at Oneida, and from him Sir John learned of the movement, and so effectually succeeded in surprising the party while at dinner, that nearly every man was captured. By this success, the enemy gained without loss to themselves, two captains, one lieutenant, eight non-commissioned officers, and forty-five privates as prisoners. Three privates and one lieutenant were killed, and but two men escaped to report the tidings of the disaster. This event occurred on the 23d of October.[1]

About a week after the escape of Sir John by way of Oswego, the northern settlements were thrown into confusion by a false alarm of the reappearance of a large force on Lake George. It proved to be groundless, and the orders which had been given for marching troops thither were countermanded.

[1] Some time afterwards, a report was brought in by an Indian, that he had seen upon the eastern shore of Lake Ontario fragments of furniture and other property that had been wrecked, and it was believed that a storm overtook their vessels and occasioned a loss on their return to their rendezvous at Fort Carleton, on Buck island.

INTRODUCTION.   63

In this invasion, the enemy upon a moderate
computation destroyed two hundred dwellings, and a
hundred and fifty thousand bushels of wheat, with a
proportion of other grain and forage, and a large
amount of property. They lost about forty prisoners,
and were obliged to abandon most of those they had
taken at Schoharie and other places, with the negroes,
cattle and plunder, with which they were encumbered.
Their loss was officially acknowledged as nine killed,
seven wounded, and fifty-three missing; but was
probably greater, although not equal to the loss they
inflicted upon the country.

Having traced to its conclusion the events of this
campaign, it may be interesting to notice their
coincidence with others that were transpiring upon
the Hudson. Early in August, General Arnold
having been for many months in secret correspondence
with the enemy, received upon his own application
the command of West Point, for the purpose, as is
now too well known, of giving value to the treason
which he was preparing to commit, by surrendering
a most important post into the hands of the enemy.
In a letter from Governor Haldimand to Lord Germain, dated on the 17th of September, two expeditions
were mentioned as about to set out from Canada for
the invasion of New York; and at the time when
Arnold's treason was discovered on the 25th, these
were both under way, and far advanced.

While it is not necessary to suppose that Governor

Haldimand was informed of the treasonable plot then in progress, or much less any one connected with these expeditions, we find ample reason to credit the opinions expressed in the correspondence of the day; that they were ordered for the purpose of creating a diversion of the American forces, and of calling off a part of the troops from the neighborhood of West Point, in order to facilitate its surrender.

Under this view of the facts, we are justified in the inference, that the details of the conspiracy would have been arranged, and the plans matured towards the end of October, and that the treason was discovered about one month before it was to have been carried into effect.

The devastation and consequent alarms on the Connecticut, on the upper Hudson, and along the Mohawk and Schoharie valleys, followed by the surrender of the Highlands, might indeed have been counted upon as a fearful if not a fatal blow to the rebellion, and these prospects doubtless led those who were privy to the negotiations, to count largely upon the benefits they might derive from them.

The documents we now publish, are chiefly derived from papers in the Secretary's office and the New York State Library, and with the exception of such as are copied from cotemporary newspapers, have never before been printed. The series known as the *Clinton Papers* and *Legislative Papers*, have been especially useful in the preparation of the present volume.

ROUTES
of the
NORTHERN INVASIONS
OF 1780.
Engraved for the Bradford Club.

NORTHERN INVASION.

Letter from Colonel Peter Bellinger.[1]

FORT DAYTON, *Sept. the* 1*st*, 1780.

Sir:

Yesterday afternoon, about four o'clock, the enemies appeared in our neighborhood about four miles N. E. from this, 66 strong, as forty-eight Indians, eighteen white men, where a boy has been by they tooked last year prisoner down Susquehanna:—attacked Christian Shell with his family, tooked two of his sons, both eight years old prisoners, the man retired with the rest of his family in his house, and begun the battle with them, and fought with the greatest spirit till two hours in the night.[2] He killed and wounded about fifteen, took one prisoner named Dan¹ McDonneld. His oldest son got a slight wound through his arm by this affair, but all the rest of the famely is save. His

---

[1] Colonel Bellinger was commissioned June 25, 1778, and his regiment included the German Flatts and Kingslands Districts. He died at Herkimer Sept. 1815, aged 57 years.

[2] See *Stone's Life of Brant*, ii, 164. *Benton's Herkimer*, 93.

other two sons behaved during the affair with the greatest spirit, and assisted the father. He got one of the death, [dead] whose name has been Matthew Bryon, and put them both in the house, gave the wounded their milk and bread, went off and came in this morning about eight o'clock. They carried seven on litters with them. The man [is] supposed [to] have, with his three sons, wounded and killed fifteen of the enemy, but it has been in vain, by the first intelligence received, I detached fifty men for his assistance about midnight, but the darkness of the night hindered them from being there sooner. Just [at] daybreak they came to the house, found the enemy being gone, then they carried the death, [dead] and followed the enemies a piece, found the field all over spotted with blood. They brought the prisoner to this post, and the doct^r found his thy [thigh] bone very much fractured, and a swan shot in the joint of his knee, so he proposed the amputation. I should have sent a stronger party, but some of our militia heard eight guns firing up towards Germantown, so I thought they might appear, and attempt to attack our fort, which is but weak in men. Then we have no other assistance than twenty of the three months levies, whereby is eighteen of my Reg^t we have been but purely [poorly] assisted all the time, and being entirely outside. If any thing else shall happen, I shall have the pleasure of acquainting you, and remain your hum^l. serv^t.,

PETER BELLINGER, Coll.

P. S.—Sir: You will please to send this to Col. Van Schaik,[1] who will forward to his Excellency the Governor.

Letter from Colonel Van Schaick to Governor Clinton.

ALBANY, *September 5th*, 1780.
Sir:

At the desire of Colonel Pellinger, I have the pleasure to enclose your Excellency a letter containing an account of a gallant affair which happened near the German Flatts.

I have yesterday been informed by Captain James Watson, one of the purchasing commissaries for the state of Connecticut, that no salt meat could be had at any of the magazines in that state, and that the order sent for that purpose by his Excellency General Washington would be returned.

It is with the utmost concern that I inform your Excellency that notwithstanding the impress warrants put into the hands of the persons appointed for procuring supplies of provisions for the use of the troops in this quarter, nothing has yet been procured in consequence of them.

I have for some time past caused repeated applica-

---

[1] Gozen Van Schaick, of the 2d Continental Battalion. He died at Albany, July 4, 1789, aged 53 years.

tions to be made for provisions for the northern and western frontier posts in this quarter who have for this month past been illy supplied but these to no purpose. The time in which Fort Schuyler ought to be supplied with provisions until the first of February next is rapidly advancing, and I have not now even a distant prospect of a supply for that garrison until the 1st of December next, and by a letter I have received lately from Fort Schuyler I find the minds of that garrison are more disaffected to their situation and circumstances than ever.

The true reason of Brant's appearing with his party before the garrison, was the fullest assurance had been given him that they would join him to a man. Indeed, from their situation, and the great difficulty I have been under in procuring only a few pair of shoes, it is what I have expected daily to hear, and they are made to believe they are to remain until their three years are finished.

I am,
most respectfully
your Excellency's most obedt.
humble servant
G. VAN SCHAICK.

His Excellency Governor Clinton.

Letter from Lieut. Col. Jansen to Governor Clinton.[1]

SHAWANGUNK, *Sept*ʳ 18, 1780.

Sir:

This is to acquaint your Excellency, that the savage enemy have been at my house this morning, took away a white woman and three negro men, and firing has been heard throughout the neighborhood. Myself and wife have escaped after defending the house for some time till the enemy dispersed,
  and remain in haste,
   your very humble servant,
    JOHᴺ JANSEN, Junʳ

Letter from Governor Clinton to Lieut. Col. Jansen.

POUGHKEEPSIE, *Sept.* 18, 1780.

Sir:

I have rec'd your letter of to-day, and am happy to hear that you have escaped the enemy. I have wrote to Major Clark directing him to march that part of your regiment — which lies on the river, to your assistance, unless he shall have received accounts in the interim wᶜʰ may render it unnecessary, and you have inclosed

---

[1] See *Stone's Life of Brant*, ii, 65.

a letter to Col° Newkirk, for the like purpose, wch you will forward to him, if you shall conceive you have occasion for his aid. Col. Pawling with his levies was at Niven's [?] Kill this morning, and if quickly acquainted with the circumstances you mention, will have it in his power to intercept the enemy on his return. Col¹ Cantine is also dispatched to that quarter to put his reg^t in motion.

I am, &c.,
G. C.

Letter from Governor Clinton to Lieut. Col. Newkirk.[1]

POUGHKEEPSIE, Sep^{tr} 18, 1780.

Sir:

I have just rec'd a letter from Col° Joh^s Jansen[2] informing me that the savages have attacked him in his house and that firing has since been heard in the neighborhood.

I have therefore to request that you will march to repel the enemy as many men of your reg^t as you can conveniently collect leaving orders for the remainder to follow you.

I am &c. G. C.

To Lt. Col° Newkirk.

---

[1] Jacob Newkirk was appointed lieutenant colonel, March 23, 1776.

[2] Johannis Jansen became major, March 9, 1778, and lieutenant colonel, Feb. 27, 1779.

Letter from Lieut. Col. Jansen to Governor Clinton.

SHAWANGUNK, *Sep^r* 19*th*, 1780.

Sir:

I hereby transmit you a more particular account of the mischief done by that party of Enemy who discovered themselves at my house yesterday morning, viz:

Two young women and an old man killed and scalped, one of the former was taken at my house and carried about half a mile from thence, where she was found dead, and three negro slaves they took with them: two of whom belonged to myself and one to my brother Thomas.

As soon as some men were collected, a pursuit was made after them for six or eight miles along the mountains towards Memacatinge, but supposing them to be some distance ahead, and our men having been without provisions all that day, and being not able to discover their tracks any longer, which obliged them to return without receiving any satisfaction. From the men's accounts, I have however, some hopes that Col. Pawling will intercept them, as he had early intelligence of their route. This affair has so much alarmed the people, that they threaten to abandon their homes, unless they get a small guard, and as I conceive their apprehensions as far from being groundless, I have therefore thought it necessary to order out one class from each of the five frontier companies, which I propose to station, with such of the inhabitants as I conceive to be most exposed, until I shall obtain your Excellency's directions how further to conduct myself: hoping what I have done, may meet with your Excellency's approbation, and I am with the greatest deference and esteem, your excellency's most humble serv^t.

JOHANNIS JANSEN,
Lieut. Col.

To his Excellency
  George Clinton Esq. Governor.

Letter from Governor Clinton to Colonel Pawling.

PO'KEEPSIE, 21st Sept^r, 1780.

Dear Sir:
  Since I wrote you last, I have received several letters from Col. Malcom in all which he repeats in the strongest terms, the necessity of your taking the command of the troops destined to relieve the present garrison of Fort Schuyler. I proposed to him, as I mentioned to you, Major De Witt for this service, but he informs me that this would occasion new and insurmountable embarrassments, on the score of rank. This being the case, I must tho' reluctantly consent to your taking that command.

  You will accordingly on the receipt of this letter,

repair with the least possible delay to Col. Malcom, prepared for this service, leaving your present command to Major De Witt. Malcom on your arrival at Schenectady, will order a company as a reinforcement to the troops on the frontiers of Ulster and Orange counties.

I am, &c.

G. C.

Lieut. Col. Pawling.

Letter from Col. J. Newkirk to Governor Clinton.

Dear Sir:

In consequence of your Excellency's orders dated the 18th September, I marched immediately in person, with two companies, to where the road crosses the mountains to Neponeck, and beginning there ranged the mountains along until I met Major Philips, whom I had ordered out with two companies to range the mountains from Minnisink road until I should meet with him about midway between the respective forementioned roads. We made all possible search, but could make no discovery of any enemy. It is my opinion, and the opinion of the most sensible in these parts, that the perpetrators of the barbarity at Col. Johnston's [Jansen's] were tories.

Your Excellency will easily perceive the propriety of my not calling out the whole regiment, when I inform you, that Col. Johnston was returned home with his whole reg^t, after having searched and pursued for the enemy to no purpose, before I rec'd your Excellency's order.

Sir, I have the honor to be, your Excellency's most obedt & y^r humble ser^t.

JACOB NEWKIRK.

Hanover, Sept. 23, 1780.

Letter from Governor Clinton to General Washington.

Sepr 1st 1780.

Dear Sir:

I am favored with your Excellency's letter of the 27th ult°, and am much obliged by your attention to my application (through Genl Schuyler) in ordering Col^l. Malcom's corps to the defence of the frontiers. Every measure in my power will be taken to expedite his march, and he has my orders to relieve the garrison of Fort Schuyler without the least delay, by the levies raised for the defense of the frontiers last spring, whose times of service will not expire until the first Decr next. It will take some considerable time, however, to collect them, as they are posted at different and remote parts of the frontiers. But I would fain hope that the discontents of the present garrison will subside when they are informed that measures are taken to relieve them. I have directed Col^l Malcolm to proceed immediately to Albany, and take the necessary measures for

collecting as large a supply of provisions for Fort
Schuyler as can be spared, for, which purpose he has
warrants to impress that he may avail himself of an
escort by the troops intended to garrison that post.

I shall take the earliest opportunity of communicating
to the legislature, (who are required to meet at this
place on the 4th Inst), your Excellency's letter of the
27th ult°, together with the several letters from the
committee of congress on the subject of supplies for
the army. In the mean time the state agent will have
my directions to make every exertion in his power for
affording them immediate relief. I take the liberty of
inclosing (confidentially) for your Excell^{cys} perusal, a
copy of the proceedings of a convention of committees
from the states of Massachusetts Bay, Connecticut and
New Hampshire, in which I am happy to find, even at
this late hour, sentiments which generally adopted,
cannot fail of producing much good.[1] I believe I may
venture to assure you sir, that as the most sensible
among us have from the beginning of the contest

---

[1] The governor here refers to a convention which met in Boston
Aug. 3, 1780, " to promote the most vigorous exertions for the present
campaign, and to cultivate a good understanding and procure a
generous reception for the officers and men of the French army and
fleet," then lately arrived at Newport. The convention chose Thomas
Cushing as president, and continued in session until the 9th of August.
Among the resolutions which they adopted, was one urging a more
perfect union of the states, larger powers to congress, and the choice
of a supreme head to the national affairs. It may be regarded as one
of the earliest movements towards the establishment of the Federal
government, if not the pioneer of this idea, which was not carried
into effect until nearly nine years afterwards.

foreseen the consequences of temporary expedients, they will meet the cheerful approbation of this state.

I have the honor to be, &c.,

G. CLINTON.

His Excellency, Gen' Washington.

Letter from General Robert Van Rensselaer to Governor Clinton.

FORT RENSSELAER,[1] *Sept'* 4, '80.

Dear Gov':

The reports of the enemy's intentions are still vague and uncertain. Some say, Sir John is coming by way of Lake Champlain; Brant and Butler from the westward. Small parties are frequently seen upon the frontiers. Last Thursday, they attacked the house of one Shell, about three miles north of Fort Herkimer. The house was bravely defended by the man, his two sons and wife. He supposed they killed or wounded

---

[1] Mr. J. R. Simms of Fort Plain, who is remarkably well informed upon the ancient localities of the Mohawk valley, insists that Fort Rensselaer was a stockaded stone house in the upper part of the village of Canajoharie, and that this name was never applied to Fort Plain, that stood on the hills half a mile above the modern village of this name. This place has sometimes been called Fort Plank, but this name more properly applied to another stockade around a dwelling owned by a House family, nearly four miles from Fort Plain, further up the valley and back from the river. It was built early in the war, as a shelter for the inhabitants against Indian parties.

In view of all the facts that have come under our notice, we cannot but regard Fort Rensselaer as a synonym for Fort Plain. The name was probably adopted when the general took command after Sir John's invasion in the spring of 1780.

fifteen or sixteen of the enemy. They left one killed and one wounded on the ground. The prisoner says, the party consisted of thirty-six British troops, and thirty Indians. Captᵃ Allen of the levies, went the next day in pursuit of them, with forty men who were not returned yesterday evenᵍ. On Saturday last, I sent off twelve boats with provisions for Fort Schuyler, escorted by two hundred men, under the command of Coll. Brown of the Massachusetts levies, which leaves the frontier very thin of men. I have also sent out a scout to Unadilla and Ocquago,[1] at which place I am suspicious they make their rendesvous.

I am anxious to hear from your quarters, and shall esteem it a particular favor to hear from you.

I am, Dear Govʳ your most Obedᵗ and Hmbˡ Servᵗ

Robᵗ Vⁿ Rensselaer.

Letter from Col. Patterson and others to Governor Clinton.

To his Excellency, George Clinton, Esqr.

We having received informations of an alarming nature, some of which we have sent your Excellency in writing, and for a more particular account we refer your Excellency to the bearer hereof, as we are destitute of authority we humbly conceive that the appointment of a committee if they are invested with

---

[1] Now Winsor, Broome county, N. Y.

some degree of authority might be of great service for detecting such inhabitants amongst us as we have reason to suppose are conspiring against us with our enemies who secretly lurk amongst us, and we further beg leave to suggest to your Excellency whether something by way of scouts will not be the best to be done.

The bearer hereof will inform your Excellency what measures we have taken, and by him we hope to receive from your Excellency such directions as your Excellency's wisdom shall direct.

We are Dear Sir, Your Excellency's loyal subjects,

Brattleborough September 11th, 1780.

ELEAZER PATTERSON, Col[o.] [1]
JONATHAN CHURCH, JOHN SARGENT, Lt. Col.,
AARON NASH, TIMOTHY CHURCH, Capt,
ARTIMAS HOW, SETH SMITH,
HENRY SEGER, SAM[l.] WARRINER,
LEONARD HENDRICK, BENJ. BUTTERFIELD, Lt.,
WILLIAM HARRIS.

Letter from Governor Clinton to Persons in Cumberland County.

POUGHKEEPSIE, 16th *September*, 1780.

Gen[t]:

I have received your letter of the 10th Inst., requesting the appointment of Com[rs] for the purpose of discovering

---

[1] Col. Patterson resided at Hinsdale, now Vernon, Vt. He held several offices under New York appointment, and was distinguished for his hostility to the new government of Vermont.

and defeating the secret designs of the enemy in your county. Before this can be done, there must be a strict law passed, authorizing it, as the number of Com^{rs} directed by our present law is already complete, and as this will take some time, I have thought it most advisable not to detain Mr. Smith, as I shall have an opportunity of forwarding the commission by Mr. Knowlton on his return from Philadelphia, or by some earlier safe conveyance.

I would beg leave to observe, that as the powers to be granted to the comr^s will be extensive, it will be their duty to be particularly prudent and careful in putting them into execution, and as congress has recommended to this state, not to exert any authority over the inhabitants of the tract of land commonly called the New Hampshire Grants, and who do not acknowledge the authority of this state, until the controversy relative to the same is settled, I have to request that these com^{rs} when appointed, do not by any act contravene the above resolution.

I am, &c.,
G. C.

Letter from Col. G. Van Schaick to Governor Clinton.

ALBANY, Sept. 12, 1780.

Sir: His Excellency General Washington, has directed me to march my regiment to the grand army

immediately after they are relieved from Fort
Schuyler. The want of clothing amongst the men is
such, that it requires my utmost exertion to procure
them, although out of the line of my duty. I should
not give your Excellency any trouble about this
matter was it not that the men are in a manner naked,
and that I apprehend, on their arrival at Schenectady,
great desertions will take place, if we have nothing to
give them. There are a small quantity of shirts and
linnen in the hands of Mr. John N. Bleecker, one of
the gentlemen directed by a late law to collect clothing
for the Continental battalions of this State: and Mr.
Bleecker informs me, there is some more expected.
I must intreat the favor of your Excellency, to furnish
the bearer Lieut. Abraham Ten Eyck, paymaster,
with an order on Mr. Bleecker, to deliver all the shirts
and linnen, he may have in his hands, provided it
does not exceed one shirt and a pair of overhalls per
man. As the regiment has not yet received any kind
of clothing, since the first of December last, it is
easily judged the condition they must be in. Should
your Excellency disapprove of the measure, my
attachment and zeal for the service, and in order as
much as in me lays to prevent mutinys and desertions,
will I flatter myself sufficiently apologize for troubling
your Excellency on this subject.

     I am, &c.,

         G. Van Schaick.

NORTHERN INVASION.   81

Letter from Governor Clinton to Colonel G. Van Schaick.

Sir:
14th Sept*., 1780.

Agreeable to your request, I have enclosed an order for the clothing in the hands of Mr. Bleecker for the use of your regiment, not to exceed one shirt and one overall p* man. This your paymaster is to receipt for, and you will please to forward a duplicate receipt, which I have occasion for as a voucher.

I am, &c.   G. C.

From Rivington's Royal Gazette, Sept. 23, 1780.

"FORT STANWIX.

"By a person of good reputation and perfectly intelligent, just arrived from the northward, we are informed that about a fortnight ago, Fort Stanwix, after having been five or six weeks closely invested, was taken by six hundred British troops, commanded by a lieutenant colonel, supposed to be the king's or VIII Regiment. Our faithful friend Captain Joseph Brant, with a party of Indians, shared in the glory of this conquest, which was facilitated by STARVATION, (*a phrase we adopt from our old acquaintance and fellow citizen, William Livingston, Esquire, now of New Jersey*). The Indians have laid waste the whole country, the tory houses excepted, down to Schenectady, where some rebels are at work throwing up works to oppose the progress of the British troops, and our Indian allies. The rebel women and children have retired to Albany, where, from a consciousness of their unprovoked persecutions and murders, terror and jeopardy prevail, even to distraction. The seditious seminary,[1] under the direction of missionary Wheelock, of attrocious name, we are informed, has lately been completely expurgated by a long merited conflagration."

Letter from Governor Clinton to General Schuyler.

POUGHKEEPSIE, Oct. 3d, 1780.
Dear Sir:

I wrote you last night, in answer to yours of the 27th ultimo, by my brother, who is on his way to Albany to take the command in that quarter. I am since favored with your two letters of the 31st of last month and the 1st instant. If my health permitted, I would immediately set out for Albany, but I am so affected with the rheumatism occasioned by my last jaunt and the present damp weather, that I dare not undertake the journey. I have communicated to my brother the intelligence transmitted me from your quarter, and have directed him to call on Gen¹¹ Ten Broeck and Van Rensselaer for a sufficient force from their brigades to cover the settlements, ag⁹ᵗ the incursions of the enemy and repel them; and I have wrote to

---

[1] At Hanover, N. H. The greater part of this article is fictitious.

those gentlemen to comply with his requisitions. What we shall do for provisions (tho the country abounds with it), God only knows. The assessments come on so slowly notwithstanding every endeavor to hasten them, that no certain dependance can be placed upon them. The cattle when received, are scarcely worth killing. The mills for want of water, unable to grind the wheat. I have this moment received a very pressing letter from Gen¹ Heath who commands in the Highlands on this subject of his wants, by which I am informed that his only dependance for bread is on this state. It is not in my power to relieve him. Your letter fully confirms me on what I had some reason to suspect, on the first incursion of the enemy, respecting the conduct of Allen. I wish this matter may be fully investigated and I beg that it may continue to engage your attention. Your letter to the commander-in-chief, shall be immediately forwarded. If the present alarm is as imminent as is to be apprehended I will see you soon if my health will enable me.

         I am, &c., G. C.
Gen¹ Schuyler.

Letter from Citizens of Tryon County to Governor Clinton.

        JOHNSTOWN, *Octobr* 3ᵈ, 1780.
Hon'ᵈ Sir:

  We are unhappily situated in this county, by keeping so many disaffected families amongst us, and it is with regret we inform your Excellency, that the act provided for sending them off, appears to us very deficient.

Many of these disaffected families are not able to transport themselves ten miles, (and yet as capable of doing us hurt as the richer kind). Others are able to defray the expenses of themselves and something to spare. We should be glad to divide what they have amongst them, so as to carry the whole off, but in doing of this, we must act without law.

We would therefore pray your Excellency, to give us your advice by Lieut. Bradnor, if there is no prospect of an amendment being made to the act soon.

The necessity of their being sent off immediately is notorious, as we are fully convinced they harbor and give intelligence to the enemy daily. We have also a number of men, who we believe do infinitely more damage than the women. Some of them have applied to go off. We should be very glad to know whether we are to provide a flagg to send them off, or where we are to apply for one.

With Respect your Excellency's
Most Obed' Humble servt.
PETER S. DEYGERT,[1]
ZEPH. BATCHELLER.

Gov' Clinton.

[1] Appointed major March 4, 1780.

Petition from Citizens of Tryon County.

TRYON COUNTY, 6th October, 1780.

The Petition of the Inhabitants of Tryon County, Humbly Sheweth,

That your Petitioners have during this campaign, labored under the most dreadful difficulties: that several of their principal settlements, viz: Conawaga,[1] [and] Conajohary, have been entirely destroyed, whereby a great number of families were forced to leave the country, in order to seek refuge in some other part, more remote from our cruel savage enemies: that still the greater number, trusting in the Providence of God, and the protection of their country, did rather choose to stay in defence of their property, rights and liberties, than to give way to thoughts unbecoming a people that is determined to be free, and would rather share the good will and danger of their fellow brethren, in the country, than to be a burden upon the public.

That it most seasonably happened by your Excellency's paternal care, which they have so often experienced, that troops have been sent up to their assistance, time enough to enable and protect them to gather their grain, whereof a vast quantity stands now dispersed all over the several settlements of their country, staulked up in their fields and round the

[1] Caughnawaga, now Fonda, Montgomery county.

different forts. That this happy circumstance, and the prospect that the sufferers could find shelter and refuge with those who enjoy their houses, whereof there is a considerable number, have been the support of their hopes and perseverance. But that their firm resolution is quite shaken, when they find that the time of the troops which were sent to their protection is almost expired, at a time when the enemy in the verge of their settlements, has in the sight of a number of the best troops, and most vigilant officers, burn'd kill'd and taken prisoners, of which almost every day brings a new instance, that your petitioners have intelligence that this is the sixth day since Brandt had left Niagara, with a large body of men, with an intent to invade our country, that your petitioners presume if that should be the case, as they have the greatest reason to believe it will be some time this fall, then it would be in the power of the enemy to destroy almost all the grain collected, besides the rest of the settlements yet standing, if seasonable and effective measures is not immediately adopted to prevent it. Your petitioners are therefore under the most dreadful apprehensions, and presume to lay their case once more before your Excellency, appealing to your known humanity, craving your Excellency's kind interposition with the Legislature, and the commander in chief, to have such relief granted as our case requires, and you in your wisdom shall see meet.

Your Excellencys humble Petitioners, as in duty bound shall ever pray.

Signed in behalf of the Inhabitants of Tryon County.

JACOB I. KLOCK, Col.[1] JOHN KASELMAN,
J. DANIEL GROS, Minister,[2] JOHN T. BACKUS,
JELLIS FONDA, SAMUEL VANETTIA, Left.
ADAM CONDERMAN, JOHN SNELL,
ADAM LEYP, HENRICH LAIRS,
NICHOLAS COPPERNOLL, WILLIAM LAIRS,
DOMMAS × GOODMAN, his mark JOHN ZIELLEY,
 ADAM CINGE, (?)
 GEORGE × KELMAN, Sen[r]. his mark
 PIETER S. DEYGERT.

Letter from Governor Clinton to Colonel Klock.

KINGSTON, 11*th October*, 1780.

Sir:

I have this moment received a petition dated 8th instant, subscribed by yourself and other inhabitants of Tryon county, in answer to which I am happy in

---

[1] Colonel of the Palatine district regiment of state militia.

[2] The Rev. Johan Daniel Gros, was a German emigrant who came to America shortly before the revolution, was naturalized by the general assembly, March 8, 1773, and settled at Canajoharie. At this period he was holding a commission as chaplain to the levies raised for the defence of the frontiers. The date of his appointment was June 10, 1780. After the war, he removed to New York, and was settled as pastor of a German Reformed Church. For several

being able to inform you that Legislative provision is made for calling out a part of the militia for a certain period for the further defense of the Frontiers, and orders are accordingly issued for this purpose which I trust will reach you before this can, as they were forwarded some days since.

The sense of the members representing the frontier counties, was taken, as to the number of men necessary for this service, and I trust therefore, that this force ordered to be raised, will prove competent. The greatest fear is, that it may not be brought into the field as early as exigencies may require. In this case, I must entreat the best exertions of the militia of Tryon county, until they can be enrolled and forwarded for their relief. Be asssured that every effort shall be made on my part for your protection.

I am, &c., G. C.

Col. Klock.

---

years he was professor of moral philosophy and logic in Columbia College. He died at Canajoharie May 15, 1812, aged seventy-five years.

The late Governor DeWitt Clinton in an address delivered before the alumni of Columbia College, thus alludes to Mr. Gros: "He had emigrated to this country before the revolution, and settled near the banks of the Mohawk, in a frontier country, peculiarly exposed to irruptions from Canada and the hostile Indians. When war commenced, he took the side of America, and, enthroned in the hearts of his countrymen, and distinguished for the courage which marks the German character, he rallied the desponding, animated the wavering, confirmed the doubtful and encouraged the brave to more than ordinary exertion. With the Bible in one hand and the sword in the other, he stood forth in the united character of patriot and Christian, vindicating the liberties of mankind, and amidst the most appalling dangers, and the most awful vicissitudes, like the Red Cross knight of the Fairy Queen, ' Right faithful true he was, in deed and word.' "

Letter from Stephen Lush to Governor Clinton.

ALBANY, *October* 12, 1780.

Dear Sir:

I this moment arrived, and am now at Col° Malcom's Quarters. Major Hughes, in a letter to him of the 10th, which I have now before me, says, that an Indian deserter then just arrived, brings intelligence, that a large body of British and Indians, under Sir John, Butler, and Brant, were the night of the 8th Inst. at Oneida, from Niagara, on their way to Stone Arabia, and ultimately for Fort Schuyler: that they were furnished with mortars and cannon, and a large number of shells, (one of which the Indian brought in his blanket). Major Hughes says, every preparation is making to receive them.

The enemy have also appeared to the northward. Col° Livingston in another letter to Col° Malcom, (also before me), dated yesterday, 5 o'clock A. M. says, he had that moment rec^d a particular account of the taking of Fort Ann, that Capt Sherwood command^s there, was summoned by Major Carleton of the enemy: he refused, but upon their parading their forces, amounting to 850 British, Indians and Tories, in view of the garrison, they surrendered prisoners of war.

Col° Livingston writes, that his intelligence is, that Carleton with his party are now at Fort George, and

90   NORTHERN INVASION.

are to be joined by a party from Ballstown under command of Sir John; and that he means if he can, with safety to his post, march to the relief of Fort George.

Thus stands the acc^t from our northern and western frontiers. Col° Malcom has transmitted them by an express to Pokeepsie this morning, but upon my informing him that your Excellency was probably at Kingston, he is gone for another express, and has desired me to write your Excellency the above acc'ts, so as to have them in readiness to be dispatched as soon as the express can be obtained.

This brigade is ordered to march immediately, and are now preparing to be disposed of as Col° Malcom, and Genl Ten Broeck shall think best, for the defence of the frontiers. ' Col. Malcom has made a request to Genl Vⁿ Rensselaer for 800 men, and intreats your Excellency, if possible, to have the men hastened on by your Excellency's orders.

The scarsity of provisions,[1] and the total uncertainty of obtaining supplies, is truly alarming. If any means can be fallen upon, to supply the troops now ordered

---

[1] By an act passed Sept. 21, 1780, the following quotas of fat cattle were assigned to the several counties: Albany, 300; Dutchess, 475; Ulster, 150; Orange, 150; and Westchester 50. By the same act, it was ordered that 2,600 barrels of flour should be assessed, viz: from Albany 2,600, Dutchess 1,600, Ulster 600, Orange 300, Tryon 600, and Charlotte 100. These quotas were to be distributed among the towns, and the whole were to be delivered before the 1st of January 1781. Of course no benefit was derived from this law in the present crisis.

out, and those already on the frontiers, Col° Malcom
requests your Excellency's interposition, as without
supplies, the militia must disband, as soon as they take
the field.' And if any reinforcements of men can be
obtained, from any other quarter than those already
mentioned, Col° Malcom conceives they will be
wanted, provided they come with sufficient supplies
of provisions.

Col° Livingston, in a letter to-day, says he is surrounded by the Indians and tories, who have hovered in
notice of the fort for the last twelve hours: that they
had not yet ventured an attack: that he had sent out a
party of 20 men who were obliged to return, the
enemy proving too numerous: that they were burning
ab' 7 miles from the fort: that they had only 60 men
fit for duty, and the enemy supposed 400.

I am, with the highest respect and esteem,
  Your Excellency's Most Obed' Serv'
    STEPHEN LUSH.[1]
His Excellency Gov' Clinton.

The foregoing is a tolerable exact state of things.
I have sent a letter to Col. Klock, requesting him to
turn out the Tryon county brigade. It is necessary
that we be able to advance with 1,000 men, the posts

---

[1] Mr. Lush had previously been a prisoner with the enemy, and afterward was private secretary to Governor Clinton. He died at No. 311 North Market street (now Broadway) Albany, April 15, 1825, aged seventy-two years.

at the same time guarded. Gen' Van Rensselaer is my only dependance. Will you come up? It is necessary. It is yet impossible for me to know whether to go north or west. *Provisions.* If possible, send some from Esopus, &c. and do urge Gen' Rensselaer to send some on. Come up. Gen. Ten Broeck's brigade is disposed of, some to Schoharie to Fort N—— & some to E——.

Articles of Capitulation between Major Carleton, commanding a detachment of the King's troops, and Capt. Chipman, commanding at Fort George.

Article 1st. The troops of the garrison to surrender themselves prisoners of war.

Article 2d. That the women and children be permitted to return to their homes, with two waggons and their baggage.

Article 3d. Each officer shall be allowed their servants.

Article 4th. No Indian to enter the fort, until a British detachment takes possession of the fort.

Article 5th. Major Carleton passes his honor that no levies in the fort shall be lost, nor any person be molested.

Article 6th. Each soldier to carry his knapsack.

Article 7th. Ensign Barrett shall be permitted to

return home with his family and the regimental books, on giving his parole to Major Carleton.

John Chipman, Capt Com^s 2^d Battalion.
James Kirkman, Lt. 29th Reg^t.
W^m. Johnston, Lt. 47th Reg^t.
Ch^n Carlton, Major 29th Reg^t., &c., &c., &c.

Letter from Col. W. Malcom to Gen. Van Rensselaer.

Albany, Octr 13th, 1780.

Sir:

A very considerable body of the enemy appeared on Tuesday at Fort Ann, which was instantly given up by Capt Sherwood. They came on to the river and burnt a number of houses about Fort Edward. Yesterday they returned towards Lake George. Genl Ten Broeck's Militia above Albany are ordered to Fort Edward.

This morn^g I have an express from Fort Schuyler, informing that Sir John, Butler and Brandt, with a very large body were at Oneida, that they had cannon, mortars and shells with them. An Ind^n deserted and went into the fort with this notice, and carried a five inch shell with him as an evidence. I have consulted with Genl Ten Broeck, and he joins in opinion with me, that it is proper to have assistance from you, of at least 800 men. I beg therefore that you will be pleased to give your orders accordingly. Unless we have reinforcements immediately, no doubt but Fort Schuyler and all that remains of the fine country on the Mohawk river, particularly Stone Arabia, will be destroyed. It is also necessary that cattle and flour come forward, not only for your subsistence but for the troops already here. It is a fact that we have no beef, nor is there either wheat or flour collected, notwithstanding my constant and most pressing solicitations. I am persuaded that you will see the propriety of marching the troops forward instantly. You know little is to be depended on in this quarter, and the levies are necessarily scattered, so that it is impossible to collect any body of them without leaving some valuable part of the country exposed.

I have wrote to the Govr this morning, but at that time did not imagine the enemy were so formidable.

    Yours very Respectfully,

        W. Malcom, Coll. Comd^t.

To Genl. Van Rensselaer.

Letter from Gen. Van Rensselaer to Governor Clinton.

      Claverack, Octr 13th, 1780.

Dear Govr:

Inclosed I send you a copy of a letter from Coll^o Malcomb, in consequence of which [I] have ordered the whole brigade to march with the greatest dispatch, and intend to set off from this to-morrow morning.

[I] have requested the agent of this state in this quarter, to forward on all the cattle and flour they can collect.

I am Dear Govr your Most dev^t Servt,

Rob^T V^N Rensselaer.

Reply of Governor Clinton to General Van Rensselaer.

October 14th, 1780.

Dear Sir:

I have this moment received your letter of yesterday, and perfectly approve your ordering out your whole brigade. My orders of yesterday were for 800, but those of this morning were for your whole brigade. I must beg you to hasten them on with all possible speed, and take with them all the provisions that can be collected. I expect to set out for Albany to-morrow morning, if not this evening.

Yours, &c., G. C.

Brig. Gen. Van Rensselaer.

Attack upon Forts Ann and George.

From *Holt's Poughkeepsie Journal*, dated October 16, 1780, quoted in *Almon's Remembrancer*, vi, 22.

"We hear from the northward, that a considerable body of British Troops, Indians and Tories from

Canada, by the way of Lake Champlain, have taken our posts at Fort George and Fort Ann, with the small garrison; and that the enemy are still in that quarter, burning and ravaging the country, in the neighborhood of Fort Edward. The Inhabitants of Tryon County, are also alarmed by intelligence, that a considerable party, under Butler and Brandt, are expected that way. When the last accounts came off, the militia were assembling to oppose them."

Letter from Governor Clinton to General Greene.

Poughkeepsie, Oct' 14th, 1780.

Dear Sir:

I have rec'd your letter of the 9th and 10th Inst., and am unhappy that it is not in my power to have met you at Poughkeepsie agreeable to your appointment. I received the information too late for the purpose.

I should do myself the pleasure of waiting upon you, at West Point, but from the information contained in the papers enclosed, in the letter to his Excellency General Washington, (which I send under a flying seal for your perusal, and to be forwarded by express), I find it absolutely necessary to proceed to Albany, and intend to set out this evening or in the morning. The almost total want of every species of supplies, I fear will prove fatal to us. We have not a single Continental troop there, and our whole dependance is in the militia, and this to oppose a very formidable body of regular troops.

I am with great esteem,

Dear Sir, Your obed' Serv',

G. CLINTON.

Major General Green.

[Forwarded by Cap' Belding.]

Letter from Governor Clinton to General Washington.

POUGHKEEPSIE, 14th *October*, 1780.

Dear Sir:

I transmit your Excellency enclosed, copies of several letters I received last night, at Kingston, from Col° Malcom, Lt. Col^{es} Lush & Livingston. They contain the only account I have, of the disagreeable situation of our affairs to the northward and westward. I shall immediately set out for Albany to employ every man in my power to oppose the further progress of the enemy, and should Fort Schuyler be invested, as there is reason to apprehend, I will endeavor to succor that fort.

Your Excellency will be informed by one of Col° Malcom's letters, that Van Schaick's regiment is left Albany and on their way to join the army, so that our whole dependence at present must rest on the militia.

The levies raised for the service of the frontiers, compose the garrison of Fort Schuyler, and Malcom's corps occupy the other posts on the north, and Mohawk rivers and at Schoharie and are of course very much dispersed.

If it was possible for your Excellency to spare some Continental troops on this occasion they would inspire the militia with confidence, and enable us to repel the enemy. The want of supplies of every kind in this quarter, will greatly embarrass every measure, and I fear that with our utmost exertions, we shall fail in collecting a sufficient supply of provisions for the troops that it may be necessary to keep in the field on this emergency. It is a little remarkable that we have not had the least intelligence from the Grants, of the approach of the enemy, though they passed their settlements in boats, on their way to Fort Ann.

This enterprise of the enemy, is probably the effect of Arnold's treason, and when they are informed that the capital object of it is discovered and defeated, it is to be presumed they will be discouraged in prosecuting the full extent of their designs, though I think we ought not to place any reliance on this presumption.

I am, &c.,   G. C.

His Excellency
General Washington.

[Forwarded by Octr 14th in the evening enclosed to Gen. Green by Capt. Belding.]

Letter from Capt Sherwood to Col. Henry Livingston.

ON BOARD THE CARLETON, 17*th October*, 1780.

Dear Sir:

It is with regret that I write from this place, but my situation will admit of no other. I have not had the least reason to complain since a prisoner, but have been used with the greatest politeness. You have doubtless heard the particulars of my giving up the garrison at Fort Ann to Maj^r Carleton, who was at the head of seven hundred and seventy-eight men, chiefly British.[1] I have with me seventy-five men, officers included, which was the whole of my garrison,

---

[1] Seth Sherwood, a captain of exempts, in a petition for relief, dated April, 1782, says:

"On the 10th of October, 1780, was informed that on the foregoing night an express had passed from Fort Ann to Fort Edward, with intelligence that the tracks of 150 or 200 of the enemy had been discovered by a scout from Fort Ann, near South Bay. And rather thinking them to be less in number than more, as generally so proves in alarms, and taking advice from some of his company, who were gathered to draw ammunition, &c. I rode off for further information, in order to know in what manner to proceed for the relief of troops at Fort Ann. I being soon met by a number of the enemy, who informed Fort Ann was taken and burnt, which I gave but little credit to, till made sensible by being brought to the main body of Major Carlton's party or army, which consisted of 800 regular troops and loyalists exclusive of 25 savages, and seeing the garrison was captured to my surprise and made sensible of the truth. And my being examined strictly concerning the strength and number of troops at Fort Edward and Fort George, &c., was ordered to fall in with the body of the rest of the prisoners."

Captain Sherwood's premises were wasted, and property destroyed, which he valued at £941 hard money.

and not to exceed ten pounds of ammunition p'r man, my communications cut off and without the least hopes of relief for some time. It is not only chagrining but heart-breaking boon to relate the dolefull tail.

However after consulting my officers and some of my most sensible men, [I] agreed to capitulate, and gave up the garrison, and consider myself and men as prisoners of war, could have made some resistence as long as my powder and ball lasted, but when that was exhausted, what men that should then [have] survived would have been massacred by the savages. This being my situation, hard as it was, I agreed to sign the articles, having liberty to send the women and children to their respective homes.

My men are divided, so as I am not able to write an exact account of the number of my men and the militia apart.

Maj'r Chipman is also prisoner here, with about forty men from Fort George.[1] Have sent p'r the bearer

[1] On the 14th of March, 1781, Captain Chipman, who who was still a prisoner, but on parole at Albany, petitioned the legislature for relief. The conditions of his parole required him to return to the enemy, unless a Dr. George Smyth of the city of Albany, was exchanged for himself and servant, before the first day of May following. The committee to whom this petition was referred reported, that as Captain Chipman was not a subject of the state, nor captured while in the immediate service of the same, a compliance would do great injustice to subjects of the state, then prisoners with the enemy, and anxious for an exchange. Dr. Smyth and family had been allowed to go to Canada on parole in October, 1780, to be exchanged for Peter Hanson and Adam Fonda of Tryon county. This transaction appears not to have been perfected, or if so, was not known to Captain Chipman in March, 1781.— *Legislative Papers*, 2,084. *Clinton Papers*, 3,263.

a few lines to Mrs. Sherwood. You will do me particular favour to send it her by the first safe hand.

I am in a poor situation to continue in this cold climate this winter, having no clothes with me but what I brought on my back, and destitute of any money. Must consequently suffer greatly if no way is devised by our legislative body for the relief of the state prisoners. My men are very bad clad, and most of them without shoes.

You will please let Mr. Gillet know that my accounts of issuings for this month is destroyed, but the number of men are about the same of last month.

I am, Sir, with Esteem your very Humble Servt

ADIEL SHERWOOD.

Col^o Livingston,

Commanding Levies at Fort Edward.

Letter from General Heath to Governor Clinton.

WEST POINT, *October* 17th, 1780.

Sir:

Major General Greene, a day or two since, ordered Colonel Gansevoort's Regiment to the assistance of the upper counties. They embarked yesterday, but the wind has since been so fresh down the river, as to prevent their sailing. I have this day ordered Weissenfel's regiment immediately to embark and sail for Albany, there to receive the orders of your excellency, or the commanding officer. I hope these regiments will arrive in season to curb the incursions of the enemy.

Colonel Van Schaick arrived here this day, with the regiment under his command. I wish he had been detained if it was necessary.

His Excellency General Washington, has been pleased to honor me with the command of this post and its dependencies. Your Excellency can well form a judgment in what state this post is in at present, in respect to provisions fuel and forage, and the obstructions which the approaching cold season will soon throw in the way of obtaining them.

While I assure you that the interest of the State of New York and the security of this important post shall have my every attention, I earnestly request the continuance of your assistance, the salutary effects of which for the public service, I have often experienced, and on which at present I principally depend.

I have the honor to be, with the greatest respect,
    Your Most Obedient Servant,
                            W. HEATH.
His Excellency Governor Clinton.

Letter from Lieut. Col. Veeder to Henry Glen.

LOWER FORT SCHOHARY, Octr 17, 1780.
Dear Sir:

The enemy have burnt the whole of Schohary. The first fire was discovered about the middle fort,

8 o'clock this morning. They passed this fort on both sides at 4 o'clock this afternoon. They took the whole of their booty, and moved down to Harmon Sitney's.[1] They have fired two swivel shots thro' the roof of this church. I have sent three scouts to make some discoveries about the middle fort at different times this day, and none have as yet returned. No express has arrived at this post from either fort. By what we have seen of the enemy, we suppose their force to be between 5 and 600, mostly regulars and tories.

V. VEEDER, Lt. Col.

3 o'clock at night. The express says there were 150 more of the enemy at the upper part of Schohary.

To H. Glen, Esqr.

Letter from General Robert Van Rensselaer to Governor Clinton.

Dear Sir:

The letter of which the enclosed is a copy, was delivered me this morning. The express who brought the letter advises, that colonel Veeder directed him to inform Mr. Glen, that 150 of the enemy in addition to the number mentioned in his letter, were in the upper part of Schohary.

I shall in an hour or two, as nearly as I can estimate, have between 6 and 700 men. Fifteen head of cattle

---

[1] Sidney's place was about one mile from Sloansville at the lower end of the flats.

intended for Fort Schuyler arrived here yesterday. I have ordered six to be killed this morning, to victual the troops for two days, and as I shall in all probability be necessitated to make use of the rest, and want an additional number, your Excellency will perceive the necessity of directing the agent to take measures for replacing those destined for the fort. The cattle are extremely small, and I am informed will not on an average net more than two hundred w^t per head.

As I have been disappointed in procuring the horses and wagons I intended, I shall immediately march to Fort Hunter, and upon my arrival, take such measures as circumstances will admit of, to intercept the enemy's retreat.

The express who brought Colo. Veeder's letter, says that Major Woolsey sallied from the garrison yesterday, and killed five, and took two of the enemy. The prisoners are British soldiers.

   I am, very respectfully,
    your Excellency's most obd^t serv^t
      Rob^R V^N Rensselaer.[1]

Schenectady, Octr 18, 9 a. m.

P. S.—I have directed Colo. Veeder, with all the force he can collect from the different garrisons, (so as not to weaken them too much), to hang on the enemy's rear, but to avoid an engagement, and I hope to be able to be at hand to support him.

---

[1] General Robert Van Rensselaer resided at Claverack then in Albany county, and under the colonial government, was colonel of

Letter from Governor Clinton to General Schuyler.

ALBANY, *October* 18, 1780.

D' Sir:

I wrote you yesterday, since which I have seen your letter to Gen¹ Ten Broeck, giving an account of the enemy's appearance near White Creek. They are also at Schohary in very considerable force. They have artillery with them, and have completed the destruction of that settlement. Thus circumstanced, I have been obliged to divide the small force that could be raised immediately from the lower parts of this county, to oppose the enemy at Ballstown and Schohary, and as yet it is impossible to do more than detach Col° Schuyler's Reg', to the assistance of the militia in your vicinity. This I have directed Gen. Ten Broeck to do, and they are to march immediately. Before I left Poughkeepsie, I wrote Gen. Washington accounts of the enemy's appearance on our frontiers,

---

militia. He served as a delegate in the provincial congress, and was elected to the first, second and fourth sessions of the lower branch of the state legislature. On the 25th of February, 1778, he was again appointed colonel under state authority, and on the 25th of June, 1780, was made brigadier general in command of the second brigade of Albany county. He held this office until the state militia were arranged into five divisions, on the 18th of April, 1800, when he became major general of the third division, comprising Columbia, Rensselaer, Washington, Clinton and Essex counties. He died at his home in Claverack, September 11th, 1802, aged sixty-one years. He was the father of Jacob Rutsen Van Rensselaer, formerly a leading lawyer and politician of Claverack, who was secretary of state in 1813–15.

and the capture of Forts Ann and George, and pressed the necessity of send[g] some troops for our relief.

I am Sir, &c.

G. C.

Gen. Schuyler.

P. S. I this morning write to Gen. Washington, repeating my request for relief, and immediately after this is done, I intend to set out for Schenectady, leaving Gen. Ten Broeck in command here, with orders to forward you further assistance as soon as a sufficient number of militia shall come in to render that measure proper. You will immediately order Col. Stephen Schuyler's reg[t] to Saratoga, to join the militia collecting there, and assist in the protection of the Inhabitants, in that part of the country, against the incursions and depredations of the enemy.

G. C.

Letter from Lieut. Col. Barent I. Staats to Governor Clinton.

Lower Fort, *October* 18th, 1780.

This moment your Excellency's letter came to hand. Two prisoners from Sir John's army arriv'd at the same time, with the following intelligence: that eight o'clock this morning, Johnson, Butler and Brant, mov'd with their army from Sidney's saw mill, down the Mohawk road to the said river, where they were to joyne the party of the enemy from the nor'ward. their strength by the acc* of these prisoners, is one thousand men, of which were 2 hundred Indians: the rest regular troops and torys. Another party of 150, were gone to Katskill. The post at this place is safe.

BARENT I. STAATS,[1] Lieut. Coll.

To his Excellency,
George Clinton Esqr.

[Forwarded to the care of Henry Glen, Schenectady.]

Letter from Major J. Lansing to Governor Clinton.

MOHAWK RIVER, 6 Miles East of Fort Hunter,
Octo^r 18, 1780, 6 P. M.

Sir:

This moment, General Rensselaer is advised by express, that the enemy are burning the country in the neighborhood of Fort Hunter. Their force could not be ascertained when the man came away. General Rensselaer intends to push on by moonlight,[2] as soon as he possibly can. Perhaps your Excellency may deem it advisable to order the militia now at

---

[1] This officer belonged to Philip Schuyler's regiment, and was commissioned, June 22, 1778.

[2] Full moon occurred on the morning of the 13th. The moon arose on the 18th, at eight minutes before 10 P. M.

Schenectady, to march up so as to cover our retreat should we experience a retreat, which we have however no idea of at present, as the militia evince such a disposition to engage, as promises a happy issue.

I have the honor to be, your Excellency's

Most Obed' Serv',

J. LANSING, Major.

Letter from Governor Clinton to General Washington.

ALBANY, Octo' 18th, 1780, 10 P. M.

Sir:

I wrote to your Excellency from Poughkeepsie on Saturday last,[1] and communicated to you the accounts which I had then received from this quarter. The next day I set out for this place, and arrived here on Monday. Upon my arrival, I found the main body of the enemy which appeared in the northward,[2] had

---

[1] October 14th.

[2] Referring to the expedition under Major Christopher Carleton. This officer who belonged to the 29th regiment, held rank as major, from September 14, 1777. He was promoted to lieutenant colonel February 19, 1783, and his name was last on the army list in 1787.

In the spring of 1778, a Colonel Carleton, nephew of General Carleton, was reported as having been for some time concealed among the tory inhabitants around Johnstown, as a spy, and that he took the route from thence to Oswego, on his return to Canada. The Marquis de La Fayette, in writing from Johnstown, March 6, 1778,

returned by the way of Lake George, and that part of the country seemed again to be in a state of tranquility. Yesterday morning, however, I was informed that a party had made its appearance at Ballston, and destroyed some buildings there, and about noon, I received accounts that the enemy were at Schohary, and it was confirmed that they had destroyed the whole of that valuable settlement. Their numbers of one division, are computed at about 600, and the amount of the other division is uncertain. They have artillery with them. Major Woolsey, who commands the levies, made a sally from one of the small forts there, and took two regulars, and killed five savages. By what route they came, or mean to return, I have not been able to ascertain.

Yesterday morning, I ordered General Van Rensselaer, with some troops to Schenectady, with directions, as soon as he could make the proper discoveries, and if his force should appear competent, to march and endeavor to intercept them.

By a letter from General Schuyler at Saratoga, I

---

urged upon Colonel Gansevoort, the importance of endeavoring to capture him, and from his own purse, offered fifty guineas hand money (besides all they might find on his person), to any party of soldiers or Indians who would bring him in alive. These efforts were unsuccessful, and this enterprising person was not apprehended. Although mentioned under a different rank, we conjecture that he was the same officer that led the expedition by way of Lake Champlain, in the autumn of 1780. The correspondence relative to his supposed presence in the country as a spy, is given in *Campbell's Annals of Tryon County* (1831), p. 159.

am informed that the enemy yesterday burnt the settlement of White Creek, in Charlotte county, and the smoke was discernable from the heights near his house. The post at Fort Edward, after the removal of the stores is evacuated, the levies who were stationed there, having insisted that their time of service is expired, and Col° Livingston[1] the commanding officer, with the other officers are now on their return. I have ordered out the whole of the militia from this part of the state. A considerable part are already in the field, and I shall leave this [place] immediately for Schenectady, in order to make the necessary arrangements.

From this state of the matter, your Excellency will perceive the necessity of sending a force, if it can possibly be spared for the defense of this part of the country.

No dependance can be placed on the militia remaining long from home, and the three months levies will soon be dismissed, so that without some further protection, Schenectady and this place will be our frontier.

I received no intelligence from the Grants, either whether the enemy have done any mischief there and whether their militia is turning out for our assistance.

       I am &c.   G. C.

[1] Colonel James Livingston of the Continental army.

Letter from Governor Chittenden of Vermont, to Governor Clinton.

BENNINGTON, 8 o'clock, evening 18th Oct., 1780.

Sir:

I enclose to your Excellency a copy of a letter I this moment received (by Express), from Col° Webster,[1] requesting the assistance of the militia of this neighborhood to his assistance.

I have called for the assistance of the militia of Berkshire county, who have attended in the late alarm, and are now returning home. The militia of this state are still in the north, watching the motions of the enemy.

I have nevertheless sent for Berkshire militia, to call on me as soon as may be, who I shall send immediately to your assistance, unless I have counter advises from your Excellency, by the time of their arrival.

I am Sir your Excellency's

Obed^t Humble Servt

THO'S CHITTENDEN.

His Excellency Govr Clinton.

---

[1] Alexander Webster was a native of Scotland. He succeeded Col. John Williams in command of a militia regiment in Charlotte county, March 4, 1780, and resigned March 29, 1781. He served in the provincial congress, was two years in assembly, and from 1777 to 1785, and from 1790 to 1793 in the state senate, and while a member of this body held for five years a place on the council of appointment. He was two years first judge of Washington county, and held other offices of trust. He died at Hebron, N. Y., Sept. 17, 1810, aged seventy-five years.

P. S. This state are always ready to coöperate in any measures to frustrate the designs of the common enemy.

Letter from Isaac Stoutenburgh to Governor Clinton.

ALBANY, 19th *October*, 1780.
Dr Sir:

I acknowledge the rec^t of your favour of this date. It affords me great satisfaction, that I am able to inform your Excellency, that it is in my power to comply with your demand, of both cattle and flour, (without proceeding to an immediate impress from private families). Most of the latter is already on the road. The cattle, will be sent on from here early to-morrow morning. They consist of 30 head of fine cattle. If your Excellency thinks it necessary, after this supply, to proceed to impress from private families, I stand ready to execute your commands. In the meantime, shall wait your Excellency's further order, while I am, with the most sincere Esteem, & regard, your Excellency's

Most Obedient Humb^l Servt.
ISAAC STOUTENBURGH.

His Excellency, }
Gov. Clinton.   }

Letter from General Ten Broeck to Governor Clinton.

ALBANY, 19*th* Oct° 10 o'clock,
in the morning.

Sir:

Your Excellency's letter I have received, with the inclosed note from Lieut. Col. Staats:[1] have wrote to Col. Van Bergen,[2] & Snyder,[3] the intelligence it contains, and an express will go with it instantly.

I have nothing further from the northward, since your Excellency left this, nor from Ball's town. If any cattle come, they will be forwarded immediately. I will deliver Col. Hay[4] your message.

I remain your Excellency's
most obedient Humble Servant,
AB^M TEN BROECK.[5]

[1] Barent Staats, appointed lieutenant colonel in Colonel Philip P. Schuyler's regiment, June 22, 1778. He died in Bethlehem, Albany county, in April 1796.

[2] Colonel Anthony Van Bergen, appointed June 20, 1778.

[3] Colonel Johannis Snyder of Ulster county, appointed February 19, 1778, resigned November 2, 1781.

[4] Colonel Udny Hay, appointed state agent, June 29, 1780.

[5] General Abraham Ten Broeck was descended from one of the most ancient Dutch families of Albany, and his father, Dirck Ten Broeck, was many years recorder and then mayor of Albany. He was born May 13, 1734, began business as a merchant, and in 1753, married Elizabeth, the only daughter of Stephen Van Rensselaer and aunt to the late General Stephen Van Rensselaer of Albany. He was a member of the colonial general assembly from 1761 to 1775, and of the provincial congress and convention which organized a state government in 1777, of which latter body he was president. He was appointed June 25, 1778, to the command of the Albany

Letter from General Ten Broeck to Governor Clinton.

ALBANY, 19th Oct., 4 o'clock P. M.

Sir:

Mr. Benson's[1] favor of this date I have received, and have delivered Dr. McCrea's[2] note to Dr. Treat.[3] He is preparing the necessaries, and will send them on immediately. Thirty head of cattle, and 50 barrels of flour, are this moment going on to Schenectady. My exertions shall be used, in forwarding on provisions as fast as they come. I beg your Excellency's pardon, for opening the inclosed letter from General Schuyler.[4] I wish I was able to comply with his request. I need not tell your Excellency, that it is impossible, considering the weak state of my body. I shall continue to do every thing in my power to forward the service. I have sent him a copy Mr. Benson's letter, and have wrote in the most pressing manner, to the colonel his

---

brigade of militia, and upon its division June 25, 1780, remained as brigadier of the first brigade until he resigned from ill health March 26, 1781. He was state senator from 1780 to 1783, and the first year of his term he served on the council of appointment for the western district. From 1779 to 1783 he was mayor of Albany, and from 1781 to 1794, first judge of Albany county. For some years he was president of the Albany bank. He died at Albany, January 19, 1810, in the seventy-sixth year of his age.

[1] Robert Benson, clerk of the senate. He died in New York February, 1823, aged eighty-three years.

[2] Dr. Stephen McCrea, medical director of the northern department.

[3] Dr. Malachi Treat.

[4] Then at Saratoga, but without official command.

brother,[1] now in his march to Saratoga, to push on, and endeavor to intercept Sir John, if he should escape Gen' Rensselaer.

I remain your Excellency's most humble servt.,

Ab" Ten Broeck.

P. S.

Ab' 150 men of Livingston's militia are now crossing the ferry. I shall hurry them on.

His Excellency George Clinton.

Letter from General Van Rensselaer to Governor Clinton.

Canajoharie, opposite Frey's, 11 a. m.

Sir:

This morning about nine, I arrived so near the enemy's rear, as to afford me a prospect of engaging them before noon. They have however, by the celerity of their movements, effected their escape to Stone Arabia, part of which is now in flames, and the whole will probably share the same fate, before I can possibly support the distressed inhabitants.

I intend to ford the river immediately, and march in quest of them, but harrassed and fatigued as my force is, by a long march, I am apprehensive I shall

---

[1] Col. Stephen J. Schuyler, appointed May 28, 1778; resigned from ill health, March 26, 1781.

not be able to pursue them with that dispatch which is necessary to overtake them. No exertion however, shall be wanting on my part, to effect it.

Two prisoners who were brought in at Fort Hunter, informed Mr. Cuyler, that Sir John intended to return by the way of Crown Point, that he had left his boats in the Ticonderoga lake, but had since altered his intended point to Crown Point, by the way of Stone Arabia.[1]

I am, your Excellency's obedt servt.

ROB^T VAN RENSSELAER.

Dubois will join me at Walrath's,[2] about 2 mile above this. I am this moment informed that Colonel Brown, who with a party opposed the enemy was defeated. His loss is not ascertained. The enemy are, it is said, between 600 and 1,000 strong.

---

[1] Stone Arabia, was the name of a patent of land north of the Mohawk, and its principal settlement was about three miles from the river, about equally distant from Canajoharie and Fort Plain. This patent embraced 12,700 acres, and was granted October 19, 1723, by Governor Burnet to John Christian Garlack and twenty-six other Palatinates, who came over in 1710. The patent recites an Indian purchase February 12, 1722, for the value of £300 in goods, specifies the share belonging to each associate, reserves all ship-timber, requires an annual rent, of two shillings six pence for every hundred acres, and has the usual condition of settlement within a limited term of years. *Patents*, ix, 83: *Secretary's Office*.

The German Lutheran Church and parsonage at Stone Arabia were burned on the day of the battle. On the 12th of November, 1784, the Rev. John Frederick Ries, its pastor, petitioned for a grant of confiscated lands at Johnstown to aid in rebuilding it.

[2] John Walrath, or Walrad, kept a ferry opposite Fort Plain, about half a mile above the modern village of this name.

Letter from Sampson Dyckman to Governor Clinton.

1 o'clock.

Sir:

Col. Livingston[1] is just arrived. He tells me provisions are coming on, both flour and cattle. I have procured a number of baggs, and impressed some good horses, and shall be on as soon as possible. Col° Hay[2] will be here with more provisions in about three hours.

I am, &c.,

S. DYCKMAN.

Gov' Clinton.

Letter from General Van Rensselaer to Governor Clinton.

Sir:

The enemy was, by the last intelligence I can collect, and from their burnings, about a mile in advance of my brigade. I have about 900 men, including about 50 Indians. I shall pursue with as much dispatch, as is consistent with safety to the troops under my command.

I am your Excellency's obed' servant.

ROB' VAN RENSSELAER.

[1] Probably Lieut. Col. Henry Livingston, jr., who then commanded the Livingston manor regiment, in place of Col. Peter R. Livingston, who resigned September 21, 1780.

[2] Udny Hay, agent for supplying troops.

A deserter who arrived this afternoon, advises that the enemy's force does not exceed 550 men.

Mohawk river, about 2 miles above camp Rensselaer, north side of the river, ¼ after 5 P. M.

Letter from Col. Lewis Dubois to General Van Rensselaer.

11 o'clock.

Dear Coll:

We are now as far as Fall Hill, Bell's House,[1] in full pursuit of the enemy. They passed this place, sun half an hour high. They spoke with some people here, and said that they had 1200 pick'd men, and could go where they pleased. After they passed this, a smart firing was heard, supposed to be at the fort, as they passed the German Flatts. I have three more prisoners of their party. No time must be lost in pursuing them. The prisoners say they have great numbers wounded; that Sir John is wounded through the thigh. They enquired of Esq'r Bell, particularly, concerning the strength of Fort Schuyler, and their number there.

---

[1] Fall Hill was a little south of the Little Falls. Capt. George Henry Bell, a brother-in-law of General Herkimer, was wounded at Oriskany, and thereby disqualified from military service at this time. He was appointed a justice of the peace February 2, 1778. A notice of him is given in *Benton's Herkimer County*, p. 131.

NORTHERN INVASION. 119

They left all their cattle behind them, when they cross'd the river. Esq' Bell supposed their numbers to be about 400. They divided at the Fall Hill, one part by German Flatts, the other by Andrustown.[1]

     I am yours sincerely,
         LEWIS DUBOYS.[2]
Gen' Rensselaer.

Letter from Col. Lewis Dubois to Governor Clinton.

      FORT HERKIMER, 1 o'clock.
D' Sir:

I am here; pursued the enemy so close, that I prevented them from burning or doing the least damage to the inhabitants. From what I can learn by the Inhabitants, the enemy is not above four miles in front of us. My men much fatigued, without provisions, I must here make a halt untill I can get some provisions to refresh them.

[1] The testimony subsequently offered before a court of inquiry shows that the pursuing party lost all traces of the route of the enemy beyond Fort Herkimer, and that some Indian scouts returned, unable to find their trail. Andrustown was a settlement in the present town of Warren, Herkimer county. Seven families were living here when the revolution began. The settlement was plundered and burnt in July 1778, and some of the inhabitants taken prisoners.

[2] This name has usually been spelled Du Bois, or Dubois, and was sometimes thus written, we believe, by the colonel himself, at a later period. The family was of Huguenot descent, and the name is evidently of French origin.

The enemy is very much fatigued. They travelled almost all last night, without any refreshment. They must make a halt.

This moment I rec'd information, that the enemy is at a place call'd Shoemaker's Land, about four miles from here. Gen' Rensselaer this moment appears in sight, with the militia.

The enemy are bending their course for Buck Island.[1]

I am, yours,

LEWIS DUBOYS.

P. S. My men have agreed to march without eating. I expect to attack them in 3 hours time.

Warrant for Impressing Cattle and Flour.

By his Excellency George Clinton, Esquire Governor of the State of New York &c. &c. &c.

To Col° Abraham Wemple, & Henry Glen, Esqrs. or either of them, Greeting:

The emergency requiring the same, you are hereby authorized and required, to impress forty head of fat

---

[1] Now Carleton island, in the St. Lawrence. It was then fortified and maintained as a rendezvous of parties sent out upon the frontiers. A portion of the works of this fort were excavated from the rock, and its ruins are still an object of much interest. A small guard of invalids was kept here by the British until 1812, although the island is on the American side of the boundary line.

cattle, and sixty barrels of flour for the use and service of the army. For which this shall be your warrant. Given at Schenectady, this 19th October 1780.

GEO. CLINTON.

The provision impressed immediately to be forwarded to the troops under my command.

GEO. CLINTON.

A Return of Ordnance and Stores taken from the British Army commanded by Sir John Johnson.

FORT RENSSELAER, Octo. 19th, 1780.

1 Piece Brass Ordnance, 3 P^d with implements complete; 43 Rounds round shot fixed; 10 do canister; 1 Quadrant; 2. Powder measures; 1 Hand saw; 1 Four P^d W^t; 1 Half do; 1 Quart do; 1 Scale beam; 1 Mallet & set; 20 Fuses; 1 Seane marlin; 2 Port Wires; 1 Cold chisel; 1 Augur; 1 Punch; 1 Seane Quick match; 100 W^t Corn powder; 1 Dredging box.

Jo. DRISKILL, Lieut. Artillery.

The Invasion from the North.

From *Loudon's New York Packet, and American Advertiser* (Fishkill), October 19, 1780.

"By the arrival of yesterday post from Albany, we have it reported: That Sir John Johnson, had, with a party said to be about 500 men, come down the Mohawk river, and advanced within six miles of Johnstown: when, hearing that a party of our three-months men lay there, he contented himself with burning a few houses, killing and carrying off some inhabitants.

Another party of about 800, commanded by Major Carleton, nephew to Gen. Carleton, came down the lake from St. John's and advanced to Fort Ann, which was garrisoned by about 70 men, among whom were 14 Continental soldiers. They having cannon with them, and the fort being only stockaded, every shot made a breach. It was however defended by Capt. Sherwood, with the greatest gallantry, until two thirds of his men were slain, when he surrendered.[1] This party also destroyed several houses, killed some men, and took the women and children prisoners.

---

[1] In the introduction (page 44), we have followed the statement above given, although different from that given in a note to Washington's letter to the president of congress, found in *Sparks's Life and Writings of Washington*, vii, 269. The note referred to, is as follows:

" * * * A large force came up Lake Champlain and took Fort George and Fort Anne, with all the troops stationed in them. Captain Chipman commanded a part of Warner's regiment at Fort George. On the morning of the 11th of October, he despatched an express to Fort Edward for the purpose of obtaining provisions. While on his way, this person was fired upon by a party of twenty-five men, but he escaped and returned to the fort. Captain Chipman supposing the party to consist of a party from the enemy, sent out all his garrison except fourteen men. This detachment met the enemy between Bloody Pond and Gage's Hill, where a conflict ensued, in which almost every man was either killed or taken. The enemy marched to Fort George, which after a short resistance was surrendered by capitulation. Colonel Warner and Lieutenant Safford were absent. The force of the enemy was estimated at eight hundred

They were pursued by Col. Livingston as far as Bloody Pond, but too late, they having retreated to their boats and made off. So far, the reports from that quarter, which we hope are not so bad as related. In our next, we expect to have a more exact narrative of this unhappy affair."

Letter from General Schuyler to Governor Clinton.

SARATOGA, *Octo.* 20th, 1780.

Dear Sir:

Your Excellency's favor of yesterday morning from Caughnawaga, I had the pleasure to receive at five in the afternoon. I am happy to learn that Sir John Johnson has been overtaken and put to route. When

British troops, two hundred Indians, and two companies of tories. Twenty-eight of the garrison were killed and fifty-six taken prisoners. Two days previously, Captain Sherwood had surrendered Fort Anne and the whole garrison, consisting of seventy-seven men.

"The invading troops approached Fort Edward, but were probably prevented from making an attack by a stratagem of Colonel Livingston, who commanded there. Hearing of the incursion of the enemy he wrote a letter to Captain Sherwood, on the morning of the day in which Fort Anne was surrendered, saying he was very strong and would support that garrison if attacked. He gave this letter to a messenger, who he had little doubt would carry it to the enemy, which he is presumed to have done, and thus to have saved that post from the fate which had befallen the others. The garrison did not amount to seventy men. Parties penetrated near to Saratoga. Thirty-five houses were burned.—*MS. Letter from Colonel Livingston, October* 12*th* — *Colonel Warner's Letter, October* 30*th*."

General Schuyler states that the force at Fort Edward consisted of one hundred and fifty men.

your letter arrived, we had about 150 men at Fort
Edward, and as many more had arrived here, about ten
in the morning; those at Fort Edward without any beef,
and those here with none but what I could furnish
them. All my cattle fit for the knife are already
killed, and I have sent to try and collect some more,
but I fear a supply will arrive too late to push a party
in pursuit of the enemy who were at Ballstown. I
have however, sent to Fort Edward on the subject, but
with little hopes that any will move from thence.
One of the enemies party who stole into the country,
and was taken,[1] informs that Major Carleton intended
to remain at Ticonderoga, and to push for White
Creek, as soon as the militia should be retired.

The prisoner calls himself Ensign, and came from
New York in August last. Another villain has gone
past here who corroborates the account, as some tories
advise, with whom he lodged.

The panic that has seized the people is incredible.
With all my efforts, I cannot prevent numbers from
deserting their habitations, and I very much apprehend that the whole will move, unless the militia
remain alone, until permanent relief can be procured.

I am dear Sir most sincerely
 your Excellency's most ob.^{t} serv.^{t},
  PH. SCHUYLER.
His Excellency Gov. Clinton, &c.

---

[1] Alluding to James Van Driesen, who was subsequently tried by a
court martial and sentenced to be hung as a spy.

P. S. The women and children, whose husbands have gone to Canada still remain here. They will be an intolerable burden to the country if they remain in it all winter. I beg your Excellency as soon as you can spare time to turn your attention to their disposition.

Letter from Governor Clinton to General Schuyler.

ALBANY, *October* 26, 1780.

Sir:

I have been favored with your letter of the 20th Inst. We are just returned from the pursuit of Sir John, though unfortunately without that complete success which I informed you we had reason to expect, after the engagement at Canajoharie. There are, however, about 40 prisoners, and the enemy have lost their baggage and artillery. This action also stopped them in their devastations, and obliged them to fly with precipitation.

Col. Gansevoort's reg^t has marched to your frontier, and this I doubt not, will give you immediate protection, and a proportion of the levies will be ordered to that part of the country as soon as they are raised.

The necessary passports for the women and children you mention shall be made out immediately after I am furnished with their names, and the steps taken prescribed by the law made for that purpose.

I am, &c.   G. C.

Letter from Governor Clinton to Colonel Klock.

FORT RENSSELAER, *Oct.* 23^d, 1780.

Sir:

The late invasion of the enemy, has delayed the raising of the troops which are intended to relieve the levies in this county, and it will be some days more, before any troops can be collected for the defence of the several posts on the river. You will therefore order out from the county militia, such number of men to those posts as the officer commanding the Department shall require, and you may be assured they will be relieved as soon as possible.

Yours &c.   G. C.

To Col. Klock commanding the Militia of Tryon Co.

Letter from Governor Clinton to Colonel Bellinger.

FORT HERKIMER, *Octo.* 23^d, 1780.

To Col. Bellinger.

Sir:

Until troops can be raised for the defense of the country, it is necessary that the militia be detached to hold the frontier posts. You will therefore order twenty men of your regiment into Fort Dayton, and the same number into Fort Herkimer, this day. There will be officers left at these posts to direct the duty and your men will be relieved as soon as possible.

I am, &c.   G. C.

Order for Garrisoning Frontier Posts.

HEAD QUARTERS FORT HERKIMER 23^d Oc^r, 1780.

Col. Vrooman is without delay to embody as many men of his regiment as he shall deem sufficient for the garrisoning of the several small posts at Schohary, and for keeping out scouts on that part of the western frontier, and to station them as he shall esteem best for the protection and security of the inhabitants, and to relieve them occasionally. Such of the levies raised for the defence of the frontiers as are in that quarter are to remain there, and be continued in their present service.

By order of his Excellency the Govr.

STEPHEN LUSH, A. D. Camp.

Letter from Colonel Alexander Webster to Governor Clinton.

WHITE CREEK, Oc^r 24^(th), 1780.

Dr Governor:

Ever since the 10th Instant, we have been all armed and embodied. Ever since our return from Fort Edward, the alarms came both from the westward and north. I kept out scouts between Fort Edward and Skenesborough, and shall continue till otherwise provided for. I received last night, a letter from General Allen, a copy of which I should have sent your Excellency if the want of paper had not prevented me. But this much he says: the enemy, my scouts have discovered them and been reconnoitring their motions from Saturday. Yesterday eight days ago, their shipping lay off Mount Independence. They moved down the lake; lay awhile at Putnam's Point. A large body of them at the same time occupied the westward shore, as appeared from their fires, and passing to and from their shipping. They moved from thence to Bulwagga Bay, and Grog Bays, Rayments Mills, and its vicinity. The last scout informs, that they reconnoitred those bays and other parts of the lake from the Beautiful Elm, in Panton, but discovered none of the enemy or their shipping, tho 5 of their vessels had been discovered in those bays the day before. They further add, that they heard a British firing of small arms, down the lake, but it being foggy they could not see the enemy, This contains the particulars. Date, Oct° 22ᵈ, 2 of the clock P. M., 1780.

Sir, As I have wrote to you before and have received no answer, and as we jointly joined officers and principal inhabitants in council, and sent Major McCracken[1] and Squire Russel, with our resolves to your Excellency, and as they, hearing of your being at Schenectady, only wrote, and sent the resolves, I can only add, I do my best to keep the people from moving off, and act upon the defensive, till I hear from your Excellency, being in great haste, must begg to be excused and remain your Excellency's very obliged and Humble Servant.

ALEXʳ WEBSTER.

Extract of a Letter from Capt. Jonathan Lawrence, Jun., to Col. Samuel Drake.[2]

FORT SCHUYLER, Oct° 24ᵗʰ, 1780.

On the 22ᵈ Inst., agreeable to orders from the govʳ and Coll Malcolm, a party of 2 C[aptains] 2 L[ieutenants] 4 S[ergeants] and 50 Privates, commanded by

---

[1] Joseph McCracken had resigned the office of major in the fourth Continental battalion, April 11, 1780. He died in Salem, N. Y., in May, 1825, in his eighty-ninth year.

[2] Colonel Drake was of Westchester county, and had been formerly appointed to command a regiment of militia in the Continental service.

Capt. Vrooman,[1] Joshua [Drake,][2] the other Cap[t] was sent out in order to harrass the Enemy's front and flank, and if possible to destroy the boats in Onondaga Lake,[3] which could it have been effected, would have been the means of the whole of their force falling into the hands of Gen. Rensselaer, who was following them in their rear. On their arrival at Canashraga,[4] we found the enemy had just moved off, and that 7 men of the party had deserted and finding the enemy to be numerous by their tracks, and the militia not pursuing their rear so close as they had reason to expect the officers, agreed to retreat back to the fort. They had returned three miles, destroying the Indian settlements, when unfortunately my unhappy friend, with the party, were surrounded by almost 500, who they discovered not until the enemy gave the Indian shout. Two of the party, after the enemy began to disarm them, pushed thro' them, who fired several shots, but fortunately they escaped. One of them was my man, who Joshua had taken as a waiter. He arrived about an hour since."

---

[1] Capt. Walter Vrooman, of Col. John Harper's levies, appointed May 11, 1780. He remained a prisoner until the close of the war, and died in Guilderland, Albany Co., Feb. 17, 1817, aged seventy years.

[2] A captain in Major Van Bunschoten's corps, commissioned July 1, 1780, and also remained a long time prisoner. He subsequently joined an expedition into the Indian country, and was killed in the battle of the Miami, Nov. 4, 1791.

[3] Probably intended for Oneida lake.

[4] Canaseraga.

Memorial from the Inhabitants of Schenectady.

To his Excellency George Clinton, Esquire, Governor of the State of New York, &c.

The memorial of the Inhabitants of the town of Schenectady, humbly sheweth:

That Col. Wempel[1] has received orders from General Ten Broeck, to send seventy men from his Regiment to Fort Rensselaer.

And whereas, the present situation of this place is become a frontier town, which we have reason to believe the enemy aims to destroy, and which we, your memorialists are a good deal concerned about, particularly when we consider the different settlements round about us. If we turn our eyes to the north, we find a settlement called Galloway,[2] and another called Peasley, who are all enemies to the country, and even Balls Town, a great part of them. To the Southward from us, we have the Hellebergh, which are likewise mostly tories, at which places the enemy may lay concealed, untill they find an opportunity to destroy this place. And one half of our Regiment are going to these settlements.

We, your memorialists, therefore humbly pray, that your Excellency will take our situation in consider-

---

[1] Abraham Wempel was then colonel of the Schenectady regiment. His commission was dated June 20, 1778.

[2] Galway, now a town in Saratoga county.

ation, and grant that our Regiment may remain at home, to defend the place, and as Balls Town is likewise exposed to great danger of another attack of the enemy, we lying nearest to them might on occasion be a great assistance to the good people of that place. And we, your memorialists as in duty bound shall ever pray.

[Signed by forty-one citizens.]

Schenectady, October 24th, 1780.

Letter from Governor Clinton to Ebenezer Russell.[1]

ALBANY, Oct. 26, 1780.

Dear Sir:

I am favored with your letter of the 20th Inst. Col. Gansevoort has marched his reg^t for the defence of the northern frontiers, and as soon as the levies are raised, a portion of them will be ordered for the same purpose. This, I hope, will give you security, and preserve the country against further incursions of the enemy. The inhabitants of Charlotte county, may rest assured of an equal attention to their safety with those of any other part of the state.

I am, &c., G. C.

Ebenezer Russell, Esqr.

---

[1] Mr. Russell was at this time a state senator, and resided at Salem.

Letter from Governor Haldimand of Canada.

From the *London Gazette*, Whitehall, Jan. 6, 1781.

Extract of a letter from General Haldimand, governor and commander-in-chief of his Majesty's forces in the province of Quebec, to Lord George Germain, one of his Majesty's principal secretaries of state; received by his Majesty's ship Danae.

QUEBEC, *October* 25, 1780.

"I have the honour to acquaint your Lordship, that I have just received an express from Major Carleton, who commands one of the detachments mentioned in my letter to your Lordship of the 17th ultimo.

The secrecy and dispatch with which this detachment penetrated, prevented any opposition of consequence on the part of the enemy: and on the 10th and 11th instant, the garrisons of Fort Ann and Fort George, surrendered prisoners of war.

Major Carleton, who has, as well as his detachment, shown great zeal and activity in this affair, having fully answered the purposes for which he is sent, is returned to Crown Point, where he is to remain as long as the season will permit the vessels to navigate the lake, in order to draw the attention of the enemy.

The reports already published on all occasions, by the enemy, of cruelties committed by the Indians, are notoriously false, and propogated merely to exasperate the ignorant and deluded people. In this late instance, Major Carleton informs me, they behaved with the greatest moderation, and did not strip, or in any respect ill use their prisoners.

I inclose for your Lordship's information, a list of the killed, wounded and prisoners.

A party of 100 men and Mohawk Indians, crossed Lake Champlain, with Major Carleton, to coöperate with Sir John Johnson,[1] who must be by this time, upon the Mohawk river, and another party of 200 Canadian Indians with their proper officers, under the command of Lieutenant Haughton[2] of the 53^d regiment, marched the same time towards the Connecticut river. They are returned, having brought away 32 prisoners, without any loss, although pursued by a superior force, of which, it is thought many were killed.

I every day expect to hear of Sir John Johnson's success upon the Mohawk river."

"P. S. Nov. 2. I have kept this open, in hopes to give your Lordship on account of the party which was sent upon the Mohawk river, under the command of Sir John Johnson. The enemy by the means of the Oneida Indians, who deserted from Niagara, had received information of the intended attack upon the

---

[1] This may have been the expedition that left the lake at Bulwagga bay, and by an interior route fell upon Ballston settlement.

[2] Richard and William Haughton, were at this time lieutenants in the 53d. It is uncertain which was the one referred to. Details of the operations of this party are given in *Hall's Eastern Vermont*, p. 383.

Mohawk river, and had prepared accordingly; but this did not prevent his success, though it occasioned him to meet with a great opposition. I have just received a letter from Sir John, wherein he acquaints me, that he had destroyed the settlements of Schohary and Stone Arabia, and laid waste a great extent of country. He had several engagements with the enemy, in which he came off victorious. In one of them, near Stone Arabia, he killed a Colonel Browne, a notorious and active rebel, with about 100 officers and men.[1]

The vessel being under sail, I have only time to inclose the return of the killed wounded and missing.

I have the pleasure to acquaint your Lordship, from Sir John's letter, that I have great reason to hope, that many of the missing will find their way to Oswego or Niagara, as some Indians and rangers well acquainted with the woods are with them. I cannot finish, without expressing to your Lordship, the perfect satisfaction which I have, from the zeal, spirit and activity, with which Sir John Johnson had conducted this arduous enterprise."

Return of the killed and wounded of the detachment under the command of Major Carleton, the 11th of October, 1780.

"34th regiment, 1 private killed, 1 sergeant and 1 private wounded.— King's rangers, 1 private killed.—

---

[1] The real number was forty, including Colonel Brown.

Major Jessup's corps, 1 private wounded.— Indians, 1 killed, 1 wounded.

Deserted, 84th regiment, 1 private; McAlpin's, 1 ditto."

Return of the killed, wounded and prisoners taken at Forts Ann and George, the 10th and 11th of October, 1780, "Killed, 1 captain, 2 lieutenants, 1 ensign, 23 privates.— Wounded, 1 lieutenant, 1 private.— Prisoners, 2 captains, 2 lieutenants, 114 privates."

Return of the killed, wounded and missing of the detachment on the expedition to the Mohawk river, under the command of Lieutenant Colonel Sir John Johnson in Oct. 1780.

"Royal artillery: 1 private missing.— 8th, or the King's regiment: 1 private killed, 1 drummer, 3 privates missing.— 34th regiment; 13 privates missing.— Chasseurs, 4 privates missing, 2 of them wounded.— The King's royal regiment of New York, 3 privates killed, 1 lieutenant wounded, 13 privates missing.— Rangers, 1 captain, 1 sergeant, 16 privates missing; 3 of them wounded.— Indians, 5 killed, and Captain Joseph Brandt wounded. Deserted of the Royal New York regiment, 3 privates."

Return of the rebels killed and taken on the expedition to the Mohawk river, in October, 1780.

"On the Mohawk river, and at Stone Arabia, the 18th, 19th and 20th October, prisoners, 10 privates;

killed, one colonel, 100 privates. At Canaghsioraga, the 23ᵈ of October, prisoners, 2 captains, 1 lieutenant, 4 sergeants, 4 corporals, 45 privates; killed, 1 lieutenant, 8 privates."— *Almon's Remembrancer,* xi, 81.

Address by the Mayor and Common Council of Albany, to Governor Clinton.

To His Excellency, George Clinton, Esqʳ Governor of the State of New York, General, and Commander in chief of the Militia, and Admiral of the navy of the same.

The Respectful address of the Mayor Aldermen and commonalty of the city of Albany.

May it Please your Excellency:

We, the mayor aldermen and commonalty of the city of Albany, beg leave to congratulate your Excellency on your safe return to this place.

It affords us the highest satisfaction, that your Excellency has, by the suffrages of the people at the last general election, been continued as Chief Magistrate of the state;[1] and we reflect with pleasure, on the prospect of a continuation of those civil and religious liberties, which we in common with other of

---

[1] At the triennial election of governor in May of this year, Governor Clinton was reëlected by 3,264 majority.— *Rivington's Gazette.*

our fellow citizens have enjoyed, under our free constitution and your wise administration.

While we lament the late depredations committed by a barbarous and savage enemy, on the frontiers of this state, it gives us infinite pleasure, that your Excellency (ever attentive to the preservation and protection of its inhabitants, and to punish the insolence and cruelty of the foe), has manifested a disposition, and exerted your endeavor to repel their incursion, and altho unsurmountable difficulties have arisen, against effecting the compleat capture of their forces, yet we congratulate your Excellency on their defeat at Canajohary, by the militia and levies, under the command of Brigadier General Rensselaer; and permit us to add, that our happiness is encreased by the consideration, that the enemy were restrained from the completion of their purpose, by the vigorous pursuit of your Excellency with the troops; whereby many valuable buildings and great quantities of grain devoted to destruction in the minds of the enemy were preserved.

We wish your Excellency every happiness in public and private life, and whatever enemies to our peace and mankind in general, may conceive from the intriguing schemes of their enterprising politicians, we trust that good Providence, which has so often protected the people of the United States of America, from the secret acts and machinations of the enemy, will abate their pride, and confound their devices.

In testimony of the high sense we entertain, of your Excellency's zeal and fidelity in promoting the public good, we beg leave to present your Excellency with the freedom of their city.

By order,

AB^u TEN BROECK, Mayor.

Albany, Octob. 26th, 1780.

Reply of Governor Clinton to the Foregoing Address.

Gentlemen:

I thank you for this polite address and the favorable sentiments you have been pleased to express of my election to the chief Magistracy of the State.

While with you, I lament the late devastation upon our frontiers, it affords me great satisfaction that by the vigorous exertion of the country, and the attack upon the enemy at Canajohary they were prevented from the completion of their cruel purposes, and compelled to seek their safety by a disgraceful and precipitate retreat.

I accept, gentlemen with pleasure, the freedom of your city, and be assured I shall always consider this act of your corporation as a most honorable testimony that my conduct has received the approbation of my fellow citizens.

I am, &c., G. C.

Marching Orders of Colonel Weissenfels.

ALBANY, *October* 26*th*, 1780.

Sir:

To-morrow, you will march your regiment for Schenectady. The following day, you are to detach the Levies incorporated with your regiment, to the German Flatts. The officer who shall command them, will receive instructions from Colonel Malcolm, who, as he has for some time past commands in the Department, is best acquainted with the posts to be occupied, and the means for obtaining supplies. You will hold yourself ready to march with the residue of the regiment, on the shortest notice.

I am, sir, your very hum¹ servt,

G. C.

Letter from General Schuyler to Governor Clinton.

SARATOGA, *October* 27*th*, 1780.

Dear Sir:

Yesterday, I received the inclosed. Part of Col° Gansevoorts regiment marched immediately, and the remainder moves this morning. I question whether the enemy will make a second incursion this way, but I have my apprehensions for White Creek. I intended to have done the honor to have waited on your

Excellency at Albany, but should the enemy make a penetration, my presence here will be absolutely necessary. The militia at Fort Edward have killed their last cattle, and I fear they will not be supplied in this quarter, I therefore intreat that some may be sent from below.

Mr. McFarlan informs me, that the Indians at Schenectady will be destitute of provisions in a few days, and that Colo. Hay gives no hopes of a supply. Permit me to intreat your Excellency's intervention. I wish your Excellency could take a ride to this place before you return to Poughkeepsie.

I opened the enclosed from Col° Webster, apprehending it might contain some information, and knowing you was then to the Westward.

The women and children which are here, if they dont go to Canada, must be removed into the country, as they cannot possibly subsist here. If they are sent to Canada, I wish Jacob Snyder, and Abraham Mills' families were detained, and that your Excellency would order it so. Their husbands have thrown out some threats, which they say [they] will execute, as soon as their families are out of our possession.

I am, Dear Sir, with respect,
Esteem & Regard, Your Excellency's
Most obedient, humble serv^t.,

P$^\text{h}$. SCHUYLER.

His Excellency, Gov. Clinton.

Letter from General Ten Broeck to Governor Clinton.

ALBANY, 29th Octo^r, 1780.

Sir:

The inclosed copy of a letter I received last night from Coll^o Van Woert. In consequence of it, I have ordered my brigade to march immediately,[1] except three Regiments, viz. Vrooman's,[2] Wemple's[3] and Cuyler's.[4] The latter as they may be soon called out to march at the shortest notice. The other two I intended to leave home, unless there is an absolute necessity for them.

As soon as I get any further accounts, I shall send them to your Excellency.

With great regard and Esteem, I remain

Your Excellency's Most obedient humble servt,

AB^m TEN BROECK.

His Excellency Governor Clinton.

Letter from Colonel Lewis Van Woert to General Ten Broeck.

CAMBRIDGE, Oct. 28, 1780.

I have just now received an express from Coll Webster from Granville, that a body of the enemy have

---

[1] This order was countermanded.
[2] Peter Vrooman, of Schoharie.
[3] Abraham Wemple, of Schenectady.
[4] Abraham Cuyler, of Albany. He was commissioned March 3, 1780.

landed at Skenesborough, yesterday at one o'clock in the afternoon.¹

As the enemy seem determined to burn White Creek, without assistance from farther parts, we wont be able to hinder them to push down.

Their force seems to be two thousand five hundred strong, to the best intelligence I can get. I got word likewise, that the enemy had possession of Castle Town, and for that reason I dont expect assistance from the Grants.

This from your Humble Servt,

LEWIS VAN WOERT,² Coll°.

The Honb¹ Gen¹ Ten Broeck.

---

*Letter from Governor Clinton to James Duane.*³

POUGHKEEPSIE, *Octo*. 29ᵗʰ, 1780.

Dear Sir:

I returned late last evening from Tryon county, and have only time at present, by Mr. Ray, who is just stopped here, on his way to Phil*, to acknowledge the receipt of your letter by M' Knolton, who arrived the

---

¹ This rumor was subsequently disproved.

² Van Woert, colonel of the Cambridge district regiment in Albany county, was appointed April 4, 1778, and resigned Feb. 26, 1781.

³ Mr. Duane was then a delegate from New York in the Continental congress.

evening before I left home. Col° Benson informs me of the receipt of another letter from you, by Mr. Chin, which was forwarded to me at Albany, but which, as I returned by water, I have not yet received.

I must therefore refer you to the enclosed papers, for an account of our and the enemy's proceedings on the frontiers, as far as it respects men, but I have the mortification to inform you that for want of a permanent and adequate force, and before a sufficient body of the militia could be assembled to prevent it, the whole of the valuable settlements of Schoharie, and a part of the settlem^{ts} at Ball's Town, and almost the whole of the intermediate country. On both sides of the Mohawk river, from Fort Hunter to Fort Rensselaer, at the upper end of Canajoharie including the settlement of Stone Arabia, are burnt and laid waste.

On a moderate computation, we have lost at least 150,000 bushels of wheat, besides other grain and forage, and 200 dwellings. Schenectady may now be said to become the limits of our western frontier, and the first object worth a new enterprise.

I am not surprised at the conduct of Congress with respect to our dispute with the people on the Grants, for upwards of a year past, it has appeared to me, that they were encouraged and supported in their revolt, and that delay was studied to strengthen their opposition. There are many however, who firmly believed that Congress would take up the matter, and decide upon and enforce the decision, agreeable to their resolution of June last.[1] The evasion of it, and the encouragement afforded to the revolters, has given universal disgust to all ranks of people, and in confidence I cannot but inform you, that the most sensible among us begin to be jealous of a premeditated intention to make a sacrifice of this state, to answer the political views of others, and of interested individuals, and I should not be surprised, tho' I may be mistaken, if these jealousies should so far prevail, as that at the next meeting of the legislature our delegates should be withdrawn, and the resources of the state which have hitherto been so lavishly afforded to the continent, be withheld for our own defence.

[1] Alluding to resolutions of June 2d, declaring the proceedings of the Vermont people highly unwarrantable and subversive of the public peace and welfare of the United States. The resolutions required the inhabitants to abstain from all acts of authority civil or military, until a decision should be made concerning their claims to separate and independent jurisdiction in matters of state government.

The jealousy with which these proceedings were regarded may be inferred from the following letter from General Schuyler to Governor Clinton:

(Secret.)

SARATOGA, *Octr* 31, 1780.

Dear Sir:

The conduct of some people to the eastward is alarmingly mysterious. A flag under pretext of settling a cartel with Vermont, has been on the Grants. Allen has disbanded his militia, and the enemy in number upwards of 1,600 are rapidly advancing towards us. The night before last, they were at Putnam's Point.

Intreat Gen. Washington for more Continental troops, and let me beg of your Excellency to hasten up here.

I am, dear sir, sincerely yours &c.

PH. SCHUYLER.

Yourself, Mr. Floyd,[1] Mr. Scott,[2] Mr L'Hommedin,[3] and Gen¹ McDougall,[4] are appointed delegates for the ensuing year, and by the next convenient opportunity, your commissions will be transmitted.

I have the honor to be &c.

GEO: CLINTON.

The Honble James Duane, Esq.

P. S. I lodged at Col° Livingston's the night before last, and have the pleasure of informing you that Mrs. Duane and the family are well.[5]

Since writing the above, I am informed, tho' not officially, that a detachment of sixty men, who were ordered to march from the garrison of Fort Schuyler, to hang on the enemy's flank, on their retreat, unfortunately, before they discovered the enemy, fell in with their main body, and the whole of them (two excepted), made prisoners. I am in great hopes however, that this account is not true, as the order given to the party, by Maj^r Hughes,[6] was couched in the

---

[1] William Floyd, then of Suffolk county.

[2] General John Morin Scott, of New York city.

[3] Ezra L'Hommedieu, of Suffolk county.

[4] Alexander McDougall.

[5] Mrs. Duane was the eldest daughter of Robert Livingston, proprietor of Livingston manor.

[6] Major Peter Hughes, a deserving officer who then commanded at Fort Schuyler, died at Cayuga, N. Y., in December, 1816, aged sixty-five years.

most exact terms. He was to proceed with the greatest circumspection, and not to hazard any thing that might endanger their retreat.

—

Letter from Governor Clinton to General Heath.

POUGHKEEPSIE, Oct' 30th, 1780.

Dear Sir:

Your letter of the 17th Inst reached me on my pursuit after Sir John Johnson, ab' 14 miles above Fort Herkimer. Gansevoort's and Weissenfel's reg'ts did not reach Albany, until the enemy were driven out of the country and those to the northward had recross'd the lake [and] returned as far as the neighborhood of Ticonderoga. The Inhabit' on the northern frontiers, from the easy access the enemy had among them, were greatly distress'd & Col° Gansevoort, before my return to Albany from the westw'd by the advice of Gen. Ten Broeck, marched his regiment to cover that part of the country, and prevent its being abandoned.

Weissenfels[1] marched to Schenectady, the levies

---

[1] Frederick H. Baron de Weissenfels was a native of Prussia, settled in Dutchess county a few years before the revolution, and was naturalized by an act of the general assembly, December 20, 1763. He had formerly held an office in the British service. His acquaint-

whose terms expire ab^t the middle of Dec^r, and were immediately to march to Fort Herkimer, to keep open the communication with Fort Schuyler. The Reg^t itself will remain at Schenectady, until a competent supply of Provisions can be procured for the garrison at Fort Schuyler during the winter, and to escort it up. A very inconsiderable part of the supplies for this service is yet provided, and unless particular

ance with military affairs, and his attachment for the Continental cause, led to his early employment in the revolutionary army. He was appointed a lieutenant colonel of the 3d New York battalion, March 8, 1776, and was subsequently commissioned twice with the same rank, in command of regiments of levies raised for the defense of the frontiers. He was appointed by the commander in chief, to command the 2d New York battalion and fought at White Plains; accompanied the army through New Jersey, and assisted in the capture of the Hessians at Trenton. He was present with this regiment at the surrender of Burgoyne, and in the battle of Monmouth, with fixed bayonets, executed an order greatly to his honor, and to the credit of the troops he commanded. He accompanied the expedition of General Sullivan in 1779, and fought gallantly in the battle of Newtown.

Like many other public servants he became impoverished by the war, and although he received commutation certificates for five years pay, his necessities compelled him to dispose of them for a trifle, and in 1787 and 1793, special legislation was granted for his relief. The treasurer was by this action authorized to liquidate his debt due to the state, upon such principles as might appear just, so as to enable him to obtain the benefit of an act of insolvency, the state taking its chances with his other creditors.

He became the lessee of a forfeited estate of George Folliott in Amenia, but subsequently removed to New Orleans, was appointed to an humble office in the police, and died there in August, 1806, aged seventy-eight years. In 1838, his daughter petitioned congress for compensation for his services, but without success. In balloting for lands in the military tract, Lieut. Col. Weissenfels drew five lots, of six hundred acres each; but the patents were issued to another party, and he probably derived but little benefit from them.

attention is paid to this business, as the season for water transportation in the course of a month will be over, and it will be impossible to forw'd it by land, the post must, in the course of the winter, be abandoned. The newspaper will give you a pretty just account of the progress of the enemy on the frontiers, except as to the devastation committed by them, which it might not be so prudent to publish. They have destroyed at least 200 dwellings, and 150,000 bushels of wheat, with a proportion of other grain and forage, though by the rapid pursuit after them, a considerable tract of country, which would share the same fate was saved. I shall be happy in rendering you any assistance in my power, in the execution of your important command, but believe me Sir, the distress of this state is such, that unless those who have experienced less of the war, make greater exertions than they have lately done, there will be great difficulties in maintaining your post.

I find Weissenfels' Reg't exceedingly deficient in point of clothing, for the climate to which they [are] destined. I should have been glad, therefore, if some other Reg't better provided could have been ordered for that duty, especially as I find from this consideration, and because the troops of this state conceive it a hardship to be obliged perpetually to garrison that post, it is extremely disagreeable to them. If the direction of this matter does not lie with you, I shall be obliged by your communicating this information to his Excellency the commander in chief.

I remain with the Greatest Respect &c.

GEO: CLINTON.

The Honble }
Major Gen¹ Heath. }

Letter from General Ten Broeck to Governor Clinton.

ALBANY, 30*th* *Octo.*, 1780.

Sir:

I wrote your Excellency yesterday, since which, I have received accounts which seem to contradict those of Col. Van Woert sent you. The enemy had not landed, but are still near Skeenesborough. Whether they will come into the country is uncertain. I have countermanded the orders issued in consequence of Col. Van Woert's information, and directed the whole brigade to be ready to march at the shortest notice.

I remain your Excellency's
Most Humble Servt.,
Aᴅᴹ TEN BROECK.

His Excellency, George Clinton.

Letter from Governor Clinton to General Washington.

Poughkeepsie, Oct' 30th, 1780.
Dear Sir:

My last letter was dated at Albany, and communicated the disagreeable intelligence of the destruction of Schoharie and part of Balls Town, ab' 12 miles N. E. of Schenectady, since which I have not been able to write to your Excellency.

As I then proposed, I immediately left Albany, in order to take the necessary measures for checking the further incursions of the enemy.

On my arrival at Schenectady, I was advised that different parties of the enemy at Schoharie and Balls Town, had left those places, the former moving towards the Mohawk river, and the latter shaping their course towards Sacondaga.

Gen¹ Van Rensselaer had arrived at Schenectady before me, at the head of about four or five hundred militia, with orders to act according to emergencies. On receiving this intelligence, I immediately moved up the river, in hopes of being able to gain their front, but this proved impracticable, as their route was much shorter, and their troops were enured to marching. They reached the river, at the confluence of the Schoharie Kill, ab' six miles ahead of him, and recommenced their devastations in that

fertile country, by burning the houses, and destroying
with marks of the greatest barbarity, every thing in
their way.

Under these circumstances, I was exceedingly perplexed. The militia under General Van Rensselaer,
were inferior in number to that of the enemy; the few
I had with me were too far in the rear to sustain them,
and not much could be expected from the militia of
the country through which the enemy passed, their
whole attention being engaged in the preservation of
their families, and the levies were necessarily very
much dispersed at the different posts, to cover the
frontier settlements against the incursions of small
parties. Gen¹ Van Rensselaer, however, continued to
move on, and being soon after joined by Col° Dubois,
with between three and four hundred levies, and 60 of
the Oneida Indians, pursued the enemy with vigor.
He came up with them, and attacked them at Fox's
Mills[1] (26 miles from where the enemy first struck the
river), about sunset. After a considerable resistance
they gave way and fled, with precipitation leaving
behind them their baggage, provisions, and a brass
three pounder, with its ammunition. The night came
on too soon for us to avail ourselves of all the

---

[1] Fox's mills were a grist mill and saw mill, on the east side of
Garoga creek, near the Palatine church, and twenty or thirty rods
above the present mills of C. Y. Edwards. They belonged to Philip
Fox. Some years since in clearing away the rubbish on the site of
the mills, some charred wheat, the result of the fire in 1780, was
found.— *Letter of J. R. Simms.*

advantages which we had reason to promise ourselves from this action. The enemy took advantage of passing the river, at a ford[1] a little above, where they again collected and renewed their march up the river with great celerity, and it became necessary for our troops, who had marched upwards of thirty miles without halting, to retire from the ground, to refresh themselves.

The pursuit was, however, resumed early in the morning after the action, and the enemy so closely pushed, as to prevent their doing any further mischief. The morning after the action, I arrived with the militia under my immediate command, but they were so beat out with fatigue, having marched at least 50 miles in less than 24 hours, as to be unable to proceed any further. I therefore left them, and put myself at the head of the advanced troops, and continued the pursuit till within about 15 miles of Oneida, and if we could possibly have procured provisions, to have enabled us to have pursued one or two days longer, there is little doubt but that we might have succeeded, at least so far, as to have scattered their main body and made many prisoners. But there was no supplies but such as I was obliged to take from the inhabitants on our route, and these were inadequate, and the collection of them attended with delay, nor could the pack horses, with the small quantities, procured in this

---

[1] Near the present dam for a canal feeder below St. Johnsville.

disagreeable manner, overtake us in so rapid a march through a perfect wilderness.

I was therefore obliged, tho' reluctantly to return, most of the troops having been near two days utterly destitute, and unable to proceed. Sir John, Brandt and Butler, immediately after the action at Fox's Mills, left their troops, and with a party of Indians, on horseback, struck across the country, and went towards Oneida, taking their wounded with them. We discovered, where they joined their main body again, near the waters of the Susquehanna, six miles on this side, where we quitted the pursuit. Brandt was wounded through the foot.

The enemys force under Sir John, from the best account I have been able to collect, amounted to 750 picked troops from the 20th and 34th British reg^{ts}, Hessian Yaugers, Sir John's Corps, Butler's Rangers and Brant's Corps of Indians and tories, and the party that appeared at Balls Town of ab^t 200 chiefly British and by some accounts it appears they intended to form a junction at Johns Town.

In the different skirmishes, a considerable number of the enemy were killed; the exact amount I am not able to ascertain. We have taken ab^t 40 prisoners,[1] recovered most of those they had taken from us at

---

[1] On the 30th of October, Governor Clinton forwarded thirty-one prisoners under the care of Captain Henderson to be secured in the provost at Fishkill. They were receipted for by Daniel Clapp, captain-lieutenant in charge.—*Clinton Papers*, 3,321, A.

Schoharie and other places with the negroes cattle and plunder. Our principal loss is Coll Brown of the Bay Levies. He by false intelligence, was led into the fire of the whole body of the enemy and fell, with 39 of his and the militia and levies of this state, and two made prisoners.

The account I formerly transmitted your Excellency respecting the enemy to the northw^d are as far as I have since been able to learn, nearly true. The little post and garrison of Fort Ann, appeared to me to have been surrendered through treachery or cowardice. Capt Chipman, the commanding officer of Fort George, having on the first alarm sent out his whole garrison, (supposing the enemy to consist of only ab^t 30 Indians and tories only), except 14 men obtained a very honorable capitulation, before he could be induced to surrender.

The losses we have sustained by these different incursions of the enemy, will be most severely felt. They have destroyed, on a moderate computation, 200 dwellings, & 150,000 bushels of wheat, with a proportion of other grain, and forage. The enemy to the northw^d continue in the neighborhood of Crown Point, and the inhabitants, in consequence of their apprehensions of danger, are removing from the northern parts of the state. Coll. Gansevoort, by the advice of Genl Ten Broeck, marched to cover that part of the country, & Coll^o Weissenfels marched to Schenectady, where his reg^t will continue to escort a full supply of provisions to Fort Schuyler, a very inconsiderable part of which is as yet provided, and unless particular attention is paid to this business, (as the season for water transportation in the course of a month will be over and it will be impossible to forw^d it by land), the post must in the course of the winter be abandoned.[1] The levies, incorporated in this reg't whose times expire ab^t the middle of December, were immediately to march to Fort Herkimer, to keep open the communication of Fort Schuyler with the country. This regm^t with the others of this state, are so exceedingly destitute in point of clothing, (notwithstanding every attempt of the state to supply them), that I could have wished some other reg^t better provided agst the severe climate had been ordered to garrison that post, especially as I find from this consideration, and because the troops in this state conceive it an hardship constantly to garrison it, this duty is become extremely disagreeable to them.

I forgot to mention, that when we arrived at Fort Herkimer, a letter was dispatched to Major Hughes command^g at Fort Schuyler, giving him an acc^t of the force and route of the enemy, and of the boats lying at Onondaga lake,[2] that he might, if he found it consistent with the safety of his garrison, send out a small party to annoy the enemy on their march. By

---

[1] Fort Schuyler having been injured by fire and flood, was finally abandoned in the spring of 1781.

[2] This was doubtless intended for Oneida lake.

his letter to Col° Malcolm, I find he dispatched a party of sixty men for this purpose, with orders to use the utmost precaution ag'st surprise, or any thing that might prevent their returning to the fort. Since my return from Albany, a report prevails, that this party was ambushed by the enemy and defeated; but from Major Hughe's cautious orders, and as I have no official acc^{ts}, I do not credit it.

I have the honor, &c.,   G. C.

P. S. The enemy bro' with them two brass mortars for 4¾ shells, which they concealed in their route from Schoharie. From some discoveries, we are in hopes of finding them.[1]

Letter from Governor Clinton to General Washington.

POKIEPSIE, Octr 31, 1781.

Sir:

I have to acknowledge the Rec^t of your Excellency's circular letter of the 18th Inst. covering a return of the troops credited to this state and also your letter of the 21st, enclosing Mr. Duer's letter, with the Information given respect^g Mr. Smith.[2]

---

[1] We are informed by Mr. Thomas Machin of Albany, that one of these was found some ten years afterwards, and made up into spoon moulds.

[2] Joshua H. Smith, who had been arrested from supposed complicity in Arnold's treason.

The Legislature previous to its rising, provided for completing the quota of cont'l troops of this state during the war, and charged me with the execution of it whenever it should ascertain the number to be raised by this state.

By the new arrangement of the army, a copy of which has been transmitted to me by the Presd^t, the quota assigned this state, is 2 Reg'ts of infantry, and one of artillery. From the return transmitted by your Excellency, it would appear, that our deficiency is 313: but least I may have misapprehended the return, or erred in my calculation, I wish to have the number ascertained by your Excellency, before I issue my orders for raising the men, especially as they are to be apportioned to the different counties, and any mistake in the aggregate number would be productive of embarrassment and delay.

The moment when I am favored wth your Excellency's answer on this subject, the business will be commenced, and I have little doubt that it will be effected in due season. I am unhappy to find that Congress have left an opening for temporary enlistments in their new arrangement. Experience has taught us, that there are states who will avail themselves of it, by which our hopes of a permanent army will be defeated.

I will deliver the information respecting Mr. Smith, to the commis^{rs} for detecting conspiracies, who will be able to make such inquiries, as to ascertain the truth of it. At any rate, it may be proper to direct his removal from his present residence. Since writing the above, I rec^d the enclosed information from Genl Ten Broeck. I have in consequence ordered out a considerable body of militia to that quarter. Gansevoort is properly situated to aid in opposing the enemy.

I have the honor to be &c.

G. C.

His Excellency }
Genl Washington }

Letter from General Washington to Governor Clinton.[1]

Head Quarters, Prackness, *Novemb^r* [5,] 1780.

Dear Sir:

I have received your several favors of the 18th, 30th and 31st ult. I congratulate you upon your safe return from your late expedition, and upon the success which attended General Rensselaer's attack upon the enemy in their retreat.

It is to be regretted that your Excellency was not near enough with the reinforcement to take advantage

---

[1] A letter of the same date, from General Washington to Governor Clinton, is printed in *Sparks's Life and Writings of Washington*, vii, 281, but considerably abridged from the one here given.

of their situation. The damage which has been done, will, I fear, be severely felt by the public, as well as by individuals. We had the most pleasing prospects of forming considerable magazines of bread from the country which has been laid waste, and which, from your Excellency's letter, is so extensive, that I am apprehensive we shall be obliged to bring flour from the southward, to support the troops at and near West Point. You will be pleased to give your opinion upon the quantity of flour that may yet, with probability, be procured above, in the course of the winter, that I may form some calculation of the quantity which it will be necessary to draw from Jersey, Pennsylvania and Maryland.

I am sorry that the troops from your state should look upon it as a hardship to do the garrison duty of Fort Schuyler. I had always allotted it to them, as thinking it would be agreeable to both officers and men, to guard their own frontier, especially when they were not continued an unreasonable time upon the tour. The frontier posts of Pennsylvania and Virginia, have been constantly garrisoned by their own regiments, which have not been relieved these two years. The troops of the line, in general, are in point of clothing, upon a footing with the rest of the army, which is very bare, and which has a poor prospect of being well supplied. But as Col Weissenfeld's Regiment is going to a distance and where he will not have an opportunity of drawing those temporary supplies which the troops with the main army sometimes do, I have given orders to have it as well furnished as our magazines will admit.

I have appointed Brigadier General Clinton to take the command in the northern department,[1] and have ordered him to repair to Albany for that purpose. I am convinced he will second every measure which may be thought expedient, for the security of the frontier.

I am much obliged to your Excellency for the attention which you promise to pay to the provisioning Fort Schuyler. I daily expect four or five hundred barrels of salt beef from Connecticut. As soon as they arrive upon the North River, part of them shall be sent up to Albany for the garrison of Fort Schuyler. I desired Governor Trumbull to hurry them on, that they might be up in this month.

I am very happy to find that the Legislature vested your Excellency with the power of complying [with] the requisitions of congress for completing the new army. I find that the Resolve of the 3^d of Octr had only reached you, and that your calculation of the deficiency of 313 men had been founded upon that. Congress, by a subsequent act of the 21st have made some very material and salutary amendments, the principal of which are — giving half-pay for life to the officers, confining the term of service expressly to the

---

[1] *Sparks's Life and Writings of Washington*, vii, 279.

war, and augmenting the number of men in each Reg^t to 612 rank and file. I therefore state your exact deficiency at 449 men, upon the following principles.

2 Regiments of Infantry, Rank and file	1,224
1 Reg^t of Artillery non Com^d & Privates	650
	1,874
Rank and file for the war, by Return transmitted	1,121
Already in Lamb's Reg^t which is the one which will be apportioned to the state	304
	1,425
Deficiency, — — 449.	

This, your Excellency will be pleased to observe, is the deficiency in figures — but when we come to take into the computation the casualties which will happen between this time and the junction of the recruits,— the number of men sick in hospitals, and upon extra service, many of the first, incurables, and of the last so detached that we shall never find them. The deficiency which there will be in the number of recruits voted, and other unforeseen deductions, it will appear plainly, that if the assessment is laid at 449 only, the regiments will want very considerably of that strength, which is absolutely necessary to make our continental force any ways adequate for the probable services of the next campaign. I would therefore beg leave to recommend to your Excellency, to lay your

assessment at 100 men more than the apparent
deficiency. I am convinced it will be found cheaper,
and in every respect more eligible to compleat the
matter at one stroke, than to have a second tax to lay.

Our affairs to the southward put on a more pleasing
aspect since the defeat of Col. Ferguson. Lord Cornwallis was retreating precipitately from Charlotte, and
giving up a fine district of country which he had in
possession. But the diversion which General Leslie
will occasion by taking post in Virginia, will, I fear,
operate against the formation of the Southern army,
and will embarrass us on the score of supplies.
Another embarcation is preparing at New York,
which, I have no doubt, is also intended for the southward, as, without considerable reinforcements, they
must abandon their late conquests in that quarter.

 I have the honor to be
  With the greatest esteem,
   Your Excellency's
    Most obed^t humble serv^t
     G. Washington.

His Excell^y Govr Clinton.

Proceedings of a Court of Inquiry upon the Conduct of General Robert Van Rensselaer.

At a Court of Enquiry held at the city of Albany, on the 12th day of March, 1781. To enquire into the conduct of Brigadier General Robert Van Rensselaer, on the Incursions of the enemy into Tryon County, in October last, pursuant to general orders of his Excellency Governor Clinton:

Present,

Brig^r General Swartwout,[1] President.

Colonels { Thomas,[2] Cantine,[3] } members.

The court met, and adjourned till tomorrow afternoon at 5 o'clock.

Tuesday March 13th 1781.

The court met pursuant to adjournment.

---

[1] Jacobus Swartwout, of Fishkill, Dutchess county. His rank as brigadier general dated from March 3, 1780. General S. was in the assembly six years, and in the state senate from 1789 to 1795.

[2] Colonel Thomas Thomas, of Harrison, Westchester county, appointed colonel, May 28, 1778. He represented his county in assembly thirteen years, and in the senate four years.

[3] Colonel John Cantine, of Ulster county, who succeeded Levi Paulding as colonel, February 21, 1778, upon the appointment of the latter as judge. Colonel Cantine was eight years in assembly and seven in the senate. He was elected to the 8th congress, but resigned before its close.

Colo: John Harper,¹ then appeared before them and offered in evidence against General Rensselaer, a copy of a letter written by John Lansing Jun^r² Esq. by order of the General, to Col^o Lewis Dubois,³ in these words, vizt.

VAN EPS,¹ CAGHNAWAGO, 19th *Octo.* 1780.

Sir: We are here, with a force sufficient to cope with the enemy, but if you can possibly cooperate with us, it will in all probability tend to insure us success. General Rensselaer who commands here,

---

¹ John Harper was appointed colonel of a regiment of Tryon county militia, March 2, 1780, and on the 11th of May following, lieutenant colonel commandant of a regiment of levies for the defense of the frontiers. He died in Harpersfield, Delaware county, N. Y., November 20, 1811.

² John Lansing, Jr., at an early period of the war was military secretary to General Schuyler. He was afterwards member of the legislature seven years, mayor of Albany four years, delegate in the old congress, and in 1778 member of the convention for adopting the Federal constitution. In 1790, he was appointed one of the commissioners for settling the Vermont controversy, and on the 28th of September of that year, became one of the justices of the supreme court. On the 15th of February, 1798, he became chief justice, and on the 21st of October, 1801, chancellor. In 1804, his political friends offered him their support for governor, but he declined. He was succeeded by Kent as chancellor, in 1814. In 1817, he was chosen a regent, and in 1829 a presidential elector. He disappeared at New York in December, 1829, and is supposed to have been robbed and murdered.

³ Colonel Dubois was appointed July 1, 1780, as colonel of a regiment of levies to reinforce the army of the United States. He had been previously lieutenant colonel commandant of the 5th Continental battalion, but resigned December 22, 1779, and was succeeded in that office by Marinus Willet.

⁴ In the present village of Fultonville, in the town of Glen.

therefore advises you to march down along the south side of the river, with all the men you have, with as much expedition as possible. He intends to attack the enemy as soon as the day appears. It depends on your exertions to favor this enterprize.

I am Sir, yours,

By order of Gen¹ Rensselaer,

J. LANSING, Jun'.

Col° Dubois.

Colo. John Harper being then sworn, says, That on the 19th of October, he was under the command of General Rensselaer on the Mohawk river: That he commanded a party of Indians on the south side of the Mohawk River, east of Fort Plane,¹ or Rensselaer: That he was under the immediate command of Colo Dubois: That in the morning of the 19th Octob' they proceeded down the river until they heard an engagement which happened on the north side of the river, between a detachment of troops under the command of Colo John Brown, and the enemy under Sir John Johnson: That upon hearing the firing, Colo Dubois ordered the greater part of the New York levies, under his immediate command, and the Indians commanded by the witness, to cross to the north side of the river to support Colo Brown's detachment, when some men of that detachment,

---

¹ Fort Plain stood on the hill next west of that on which the Female Seminary stands, about half a mile west of the present village of Fort Plain, and on the south side of the Mohawk river.

which had been defeated and dispersed, came to the river and crossed it, and gave the deponent information of the state of Colo. Brown's party.

That upon hearing that Colo. Brown was defeated, the deponent informed Colo. Dubois of the disaster, and that the whole of the detachm^t of levies and Indians or part of them, who had crossed to support Colo. Brown, recrossed to the south side.

That Colo. Dubois then informed the deponent that General Rensselaer was below, and requested him to ride down to the Genl and advise him of the fate of Brown's detachment, which he accordingly did.

That he found General Rensselaer halted about a mile below Fort Rensselaer.

That he entreated the general to march on: That he informed him there was a ford near at hand, about knee deep, where the troops might cross: That he urged the general to attack the enemy at all events: That the general informed him he did not know the enemy's numbers, nor the route they intended to take: That he told the general that if the enemy took the same route which they did when they came, they could do us no more injury than they had already done, or if he should go thro' Johnstown, they would hurt their friends and not ours.

That the general then told him, that he would go to Colo. Dubois and advise with him, and that he attended the general there: That he is ignorant of what passed between Colo. Dubois and the general, but that the levies and Indians with some of the Tryon county militia, recrossed to the north side of the river, either by the generals', or Colo Dubois' orders: — the deponent supposed it to have been by the Gen¹ˢ order.

That while the detachment under Col. Dubois, and the Indians & militia were crossing, the Gen¹ and Colo Dubois went to Fort Rensselaer and there dined. That they returned to the bank of the river, and there stood at the ferry[1] for a considerable time after the levies and Indians had crossed: That the deponent came to the north bank of the river and hailed the Gen¹, intreating him for God's sake to cross, but he rec⁴ no reply.

That the deponent believes the levies and Indians had all crossed about 1 o'clock, and that he believes it was near three hours thereafter, before the immediate command of Genl. Rensselaer, (who had crossed about a mile below), came up to the ferry, where the levies and Indians remained paraded.

That when the militia came up, the whole of the troops were divided into three columns, and marched to attack the enemy. Colo Dubois with the levies on the right the Albany militia on the left and that he does not know who commanded the central column, composed of whites and Indians. That the deponent commanded the Indians, in advance of the centre column.

[1] John Walrod's ferry, opposite Fort Plain.

That after advancing some distance, he was met by
an Indian who informed him that the enemy were
near at hand, and that the enemy's force was about
four hundred white men, and but few Indians; which
the deponent in person immediately communicated to
Gen¹ Rensselaer, then at the head of the centre column,
and then returned to his command, without receiving
any further orders from the general. That after
advancing about half a mile, his party fell in with,
and began to skirmish with the enemy's rear guard,
who were then retreating up the river. That part of
the centre column also fell in with that part of the
enemy. That the enemy then changed their front,
came down the river and engaged our left, and commenced a regular and heavy platoon firing on them:
But that our left, not being pressed, fired irregularly,
and were beat back, but advanced again and continued firing irregularly. That at this juncture, the
enemy attempted to gain and secure the ford. That
thereupon part of the centre column, filed off to the
right and joined Colo. Dubois' detachm' who attempted
to gain the enemy's left flank, and the remainder continued, with five of the Indians, advancing in the
centre. That soon after a heavy fire commenced, and
was continued on the right, which the deponent has
since been informed, happened between Colo Whiting¹
and the enemy. That when the firing on the right

---

¹ William W. Whiting, commissioned colonel June 16, 1778.

commenced, it was quite dusk, and the detachment under Colo Dubois had gained the enemy's left, and they were fording the river.

That he was then informed by Colo Dubois, that the general had ordered a retreat, and was requested by the Colonel to communicate it to Major Benschoten.[1] That he did not receive orders to retire, till the enemy had crossed to the south side of the river. That when he went in search of Major Benschoten, he found some of the troops composed of Tryon militia and levies, plundering. That he forbid it, and ordered the Indians to remain in close quarters, least some accident might happen to them.

Question by the Genl. How was you informed that the enemy had crossed?

Answer. When I was in quest of Major Benschoten, I was informed by many people, who were on the ground, that the enemy had crossed.

Quest. Did you see me after that?

Ans^r. No, sir.

Quest. Did you send me any information that the enemy had crossed the river?

Ans^r. I did not.

Quest. Did our troops engage the enemy as they were first formed and advanced?

Ans^r. No.

---

[1] Elias Van Buntschoten was appointed major in Colonel Dubois's regiment raised for the defence of the frontiers, July 1, 1780.

Quest. Do you not recollect that you came to me before the skirmishing began, and requested that the Indians might go in the rear of the centre column?

Ans^r. I do not.

Quest. Did you observe the militia on the left to be in great confusion, when the firing commenced?

Ans^r. I did.

Mr. Wm Harper,[1] being sworn, says, That he was at Schenectady on the evening of the 17th October, when Genl Rensselaer arrived there with the militia, and they discovered the lights of fires at the lower end of Schoharie, where they had received information that the enemy were burning. That he was informed the militia under the general were to march the next morning. That the militia remained in Schenectady till it was late in the morning. That the deponent being impatient, went on to the Williger, about fourteen miles above Schenectady, where he received information that the enemy were burning at the Cadorotty[2] about a mile above Fort Hunter. That the express who came from Fort Hunter, to Genl

---

[1] "William Harper was an active member of the provincial congress, and after the war, was six years a member of the state legislature. When Otsego county was formed, he was appointed one of the assistant judges. He lived to a great age, and died a few years since at Milford, in Otsego county, retaining to the last that strong desire for information which had characterized his public life." — *Annals of Tryon County*, ed. of 1831, p. 155.

[2] A mile or two up Schoharie creek on the east side. Sometimes spelled *Cadaughrita*.

Rensselaer was forwarded by the Dep^t, that the Genl and troops soon came on. That it was near sunset when they rec^d information of the enemy's being at Warrensbush.[1] That the troops were ordered to halt at Elliott's at the Old Farms.

That the Genl applied to the deponent, to procure a reconnoitering party to discover the number, situation and movements of the enemy. That he procured them and waited on the Genl. That the Genl told him he would consult with his field officers, and that thereupon he sent a Sergeant, Wm Wood, with seven or eight men to reconnoitre the enemy. That the depon^t accompanied the party to Fort Hunter, and from thence, he with one man went to Anthony's Nose, where the enemy had their camp. That they returned with all possible dispatch to the General, whom they found advanced with the troops as far as Gardinier's Flatts,[2] about four and a half miles above Fort Hunter, and twenty-six above Schenectady, about twelve o'clock at night or after.

That he informed the general of the enemy's situation, and that the Genl continued advancing with the troops to Van Eps, about half or three fourths of a mile.

---

[1] Warrensbush was the name applied to a tract of some fifteen thousand acres of land mostly in the present town of Florida, Montgomery county, owned by Sir Peter Warren, an uncle of Sir William Johnson.

[2] A short distance below Fultonville.

That the Gen¹ then ordered letters to be written to the officers commanding at Fort Plane or Rensselaer, and Stone Arabia and they were given in charge to Lt Wm Wallace. That the Gen¹ and troops remained at Van Ep's between two and three hours, and that soon after the march the day broke. That the troops marched about four miles, to Peter Lewis'[1] where the whole halted about ten or twelve minutes for the purpose of examining a prisoner taken by our advance party. That the troops were marched two or three miles to Putnam's Lands, where the whole body halted a considerable time, and the advance party were on or near the ground where the enemy had halted that night. That the deponent went to the Gen¹ and urged to him that the troops might be ordered to march, but the Gen¹ answered that he must first furnish the troops with cartridges. That soon after leave was obtained for Major McKinster with the advance party to march.

That while the troops were halted there, Col. Louis[2] had been sent out to reconnoitre whether the enemy did not remain at the Nose, to ambuscade Gen¹ Rensselaer's troops.

---

[1] At Stone Ridge, near the west line of the town of Glen.

[2] Col. Louis Cook, an Indian from Caughnawaga village, near Montreal, who had joined the American army, and had received a commission as lieutenant colonel. His Indian name was Atiatonharonkwen. He afterwards lived at St. Regis. He died near Buffalo, towards the close of the war of 1812-15.— *Hough's History of St. Lawrence and Franklin Counties,* p. 182.

That the advance party under Major McKinster,[1] marched on to lame Corn⁸ Van Alstyne's, and that he and the major discovered the enemy drawn upon the opposite side of the river at John Saxe's house. That the road at the Nose was very bad, so as to render it difficult to come up with artillery. That Major McKinster's party halted about an hour at Van Alstyne's before the main body came up. That as soon as the main body arrived, the whole marched about a mile, to another Corn⁸ Van Alstyne's: and on their arrival there they heard a firing between Col° Browns detachment and the enemy.

That the Gen¹ enquired from the deponent the best place to ford the river. That upon trial at Major Yale's it was found impracticable. That they then marched on to Adam Countryman's ab¹ one and a

---

[1] Col. John Mc Kinstry served with reputation through the war, in which he was repeatedly and severely wounded, and some of the enemy's balls he carried with him to the grave. He was appointed a major in Col. Van Ess's regiment on the 28th of May, 1778, and served in this capacity in the Mohawk campaign of 1780. At the battle of the Cedars, on the St. Lawrence, while serving as captain in Col. Patterson's regiment, he was twice wounded and taken prisoner by the Indians. Being selected for torture, he was bound to a tree and surrounded by faggots, but as the torch was about to be applied, he was ransomed and rescued by Brant, who recognized a masonic sign given by the prisoner. A warm friendship sprung up from this incident, and Brant repeatedly visited his protege after the war.

Colonel Mc Kinstry retired to his farm in Livingston, Columbia county, after the war, represented his county two years in assembly, and died on the 9th of June, 1822, aged 77 years. — *Albany Gazette*, June 18, 1822; *Stone's Life of Brant*, i, 155, ii, 490.

half miles, where the whole of the troops halted and another party was ordered to advance.

That the troops had been there about half an hour when Col° Harper[1] came to the Gen¹ and gave him an acco¹ of Colo Brown's disaster.

That it was full three hours from that time, before the troops under Gen¹ Rensselaer crossed and came up to Walrod's Ferry. That Gen¹ Rensselaer went up to Walrod's Ferry on the south side of the river, but when the deponent knows not.

That the General stood at the ferry, and was pressed and intreated by him, Colo Harper and others to cross the river, and attack the enemy, but that he gave no answer, nor came over, till his militia had joined Colo. Dubois' command.

That after the troops had joined, they were divided into three columns, the right commanded by Colo Dubois. That about sunset or after, the enemy came down out of the woods to Philan's orchard, when a skirmishing began between our left and the enemy in the lowlands. That our left was much disordered, and fired very irregularly and never were in order after the firing commenced.

That the rear of our left was about five hundred yards from the enemy when the front began their firing at about two hundred and fifty and the whole kept up a brisk fire towards the enemy. That he saw

[1] Colonel John Harper.

several officers (and particularly Adj^t Van Veghten[1] of Colo Cuylers reg't), exert themselves to bring on the troops, and to prevent their running away, but that they were not able to bring up the men so close to action as to annoy the enemy.

That the confusion took place as soon as the firing commenced, and that it was pretty dark before it ceased. That about the time when the firing on our part ceased, the Dep^t saw the Genl with the left column. That the Genl informed him, that as it was dark, and dangerous to let the firing continue, least our troops should kill each other, he had ordered, or would order the troops out of action. That he pressed the Genl to push the enemy while they were crossing the river, but the Genl declined it. That it was then dark.

That the General observed to the Deponent, that he was apprehensive that the enemy would surround our troops, and desired the deponent to ride down to the river and inform himself whether the enemy were not attempting it. That he replied to the Genl, they were crossing the river, but in compliance with the General's request he rode down.

That the place where the enemy crossed the river is a common ford and generally made use of. That when the Genl told him, he was resolved to call the

---

[1] Hendrick Van Veghten was appointed adjutant in Colonel Abraham Cuyler's regiment, April 4, 1778.

men off, he requested the Gen¹ to encamp there on the low ground, the field of action. But that the General replied he would go to the hills, and he with the troops retired to a hill about a mile from the field of action.

Henry Glen Esqʳ being sworn, says: That on the 17th Octʳ about 5 o'clock P. M. General Rensselaer arrived at Schenectady at the deponent's house, and informed him that a number of troops were on their march from Albany. That the Gen¹ appeared solicitous to procure horses to mount his troops on, and expedite their march to Fort Hunter, to waylay the enemy who were on their way from Schoharie to the Mohawk river.

That the Deponent as acting quartermaster of the Department advised the Gen¹ that the most eligible mode of procuring horses would be by having the inhabitants of Schenectady convened, which was accordingly done in the evening. That the Gen¹ then represented to the inhabitants that he wanted four or five hundred horses to mount his men on, to go to Fort Hunter, for the purpose above mentioned.

That the Gen¹ informed the inhabitants, that the deponent had received an express from Colº Veeder commanding the lower fort at Schoharie, informing him that the enemy had burnt and destroyed the settlements at Schoharie, on that day, and were halted that night at one Sidney's,[1] about fourteen or sixteen

---
[1] In the present town of Esperance.

miles from Fort Hunter. That the distance from Schenectady to Fort Hunter is twenty miles. That the few inhabitants who were collected, promised the general their horses, and that they should be sent to the deponent's house by break of day, next morning. That it was also proposed by Gen¹ Rensselaer, that in case a sufficiency of horses could not be procured, he would take waggons to carry the greater number of the men on.

Quest. by Gen¹ Rensselaer. Were the horses or waggons ready as I had required?

Ans. They were not.

Quest. Do you recollect, that as soon as I arrived at Schenectady, I went to the commissary, and desired him to procure, or get in readiness that evening, provisions for the troops who were coming on?

Ans. I do. But the commissary had no provisions. He sent out and procured two beeves, which were killed the next morning, but it was late before the troops were served. The last drew their rations about eight o'clock.

Quest. Do you recollect my sending that night to Col° Van Alstyne[1] who was at Nestigona[2] to expedite

---

[1] Abraham Van Alstyne was appointed colonel, April 2, 1773.

[2] Nestigione is the name of a land patent, in Saratoga county, granted to John Rosie and others, April 22, 1708. It lay in the rear of a row of farms fronting the river, and was a mile in depth, in the present county of Saratoga. The name is sometimes found written *Connestigone*, or *Niskayuna*; the latter now limited to a township south of the Mohawk in Schenectady county.

his march so as to be in town by daylight next morning?

Ans. I do.

Quest. After the troops were served with provisions, did I, to your knowledge, make any unnecessary delay in marching thus?

Ans. You did not.

Quest. What distance is it, between Nestigiona and Sir William Johnson's old place?

Ans. The distance between its nearest settlement called Rosendal and Sir W$^{m's}$ old place is about nineteen miles.

Quest. Had the troops any time to cook their provisions, from the time they drew it till their march?

Ans. They had not.

Court: *Quest.* Had you any intelligence from Gen. Rensselaer on the day of his march, after he left Schenectady.

Ans. Yes. The same evening an express came from the Genl with a letter to the governor dated at Chucktinunda,[1] six miles east of Fort Hunter informing the Govr that he had halted to refresh his men, till moon rise, when he intended to march. Afterwards an express from the officer commanding at Fort

---

[1] The Chuctanunda creek unites with the Mohawk opposite the present village of Amsterdam. The road south of the river, in former times, instead of following the bend of the river, here passed up over the hill, and thence in a direct line to Fort Hunter. This road was about five miles long, and passed nearly two miles from the river.

Hunter came to me, with an acco' that Sir John Johnson had that afternoon passed Fort Hunter and had destroyed Cadorothy on his route.

Quest. Are you acquainted with the roads and passes of Cheektinunda Hill?

Ans. I am. The road is bad, and up a long clay hill with a pretty close wood on both sides.

Colo. Lewis Dubois, being duly sworn, says, that on the 19th October last, at about two o'clock p. m., he met General Rensselaer about three-fourths of a mile below Fort Rensselaer, and informed him that Colo. Brown was defeated, and that the enemy were advancing up the river. That the general then advised with him where would be the most convenient spot to meet them: that he told the general there was a fording place just by the ground where the troops then were, and that in case they crossed there, it would expedite the pursuit after the enemy more than if they crossed in the two small boats above, which would delay them a long time.

That the general then gave orders to Lt. Driskill to send the artillery to Fort Rensselaer, and that the troops should cross immediately. That the deponent then asked the general whether he had dined. The general replied that he had not. That as soon as the general had put the troops in motion, he rode to the deponent's quarters in Fort Rensselaer to take dinner, after leaving orders with the officers to cross the river with all possible dispatch.

That Lt. Driskill was then ordered to leave his men in Fort Rensselaer, to work the artillery in case the enemy should attack it, and some of the militia who were in the fort, were ordered to cross the river, and Mr. Lansing was sent down by the general to expedite the crossing of the militia.

That the Gen¹ and the deponent then went down to Wolrod's ferry, and found that the militia had not yet come up. That he sent several expresses to hurry them on. That upon their coming to the ferry, they found several of the militia who had not yet crossed, but immediately passed the ferry, and then the Gen¹ and the deponent crossed as quick as possible. That about the time of their crossing, they discovered from the firing, that the enemy were coming down out of the woods towards the river, at or near Fox's Mills. That shortly thereafter Gen¹ Rensselaer's militia joined, and the general advised with him on the most eligible mode of attacking the enemy. That the plan of attack was directed to be in three columns. The right composed of levies commanded by the deponent, to be on the high ground; the left composed of militia, and commanded by Colᵒ Cuyler, to be on the low ground, and the centre to be commanded by Colo. Whiting.

That it was found inconvenient to march in columns and they were ordered to subdivide into sections and so marched on till they came in sight of the enemy. That the deponent rode down to the Gen¹ (then in the centre column) and informed him that the enemy were formed as follows: That their rangers were on their right, on the bank of the river, the regular troops in the centre on the flatts in column, and the Indians and riflemen on the left, about 150 yards advanced of the other troops, in an orchard near Klock's house.

That upon reconnoitering the ground, it was found impracticable to form the centre and left columns as was first intended. That they were therefore subdivided into smaller detachments. That thereupon a skirmishing commenced between some scattering Indians and white men, advanced of the right of the centre column of the enemy. That the deponent then retired to his command. That Major McKinstry in pursuance of the General's orders, filed off to the right from the centre and marched very near the right column.

That the remainder of the centre column under the command of Colo Whiting, advanced to the orchard at Klock's house and engaged them. That the firing on the part of the enemy was so warm, as to prevent troops under Colo Whiting from advancing. That thereupon the deponent ordered two companies of his column to raise the summit of the hill and fire on the enemy in flank, which broke them and they ran off. That the deponent then marched on till he gained the flank of the enemy's main body, pursuant to the General's order. That it began to grow dusk and he discovered that his front had got into the enemy's rear. That thereupon, he faced his men about, and marched in a line down to the enemy undiscovered: That he gave orders for firing platoons from right to left, when the enemy broke and ran: That he advanced and continued firing upon the enemy till he discovered a firing on the rear of his left. That finding it came from some part of our own militia, he halted his men and rode up to the militia, and met with General Rensselaer on the left of the centre column, where he found the militia had given way.

That it was so dark that he could not discover Gen¹ Rensselaer at the distance of five paces, nor know him but from his voice, and that when he came up to the Gen¹ he found his efforts in vain. That he informed the Gen¹ that the right of the centre line were firing on the levies, who were advanced against the enemy. That it was then proposed by either the Gen¹ or the deponent, that the firing should be ordered to cease, least our men should kill each other.

That the Gen¹ requested him to ride to the rear of the troops and stop their retreating, and inform them that the enemy had retired over the river. That he went some distance, and on his return informed the Gen¹ that he could not overtake the fronts. That the Gen¹ inquired from him, whether he knew of a good piece of ground to encamp on that night. That he thereupon recommended a hill near Klock's house, and an order was sent to Major Benschoten of the levies to return to the ground near Klock's house.

That on riding with the Genl he mentioned his apprehensions, that his men would want provisions for the march the next day. That the deponent then recommended to the Genl a spot of ground near Fox's where the troops would be secure from surprise and provisions might be brought to them from the baggage waggons which were at Fort Rensselaer. That part of the levies were left at Klock's house, to take charge of the wounded, and of the stores taken from the enemy, and the remainder of the troops retired to Fox's.

That the Genl immediately ordered parties to Fort Rensselaer for provisions for the militia, and ordered the deponent to hold himself and the levies in readiness to march before daylight the next morning in pursuit of the enemy. That in consequence thereof, he marched with the troops about 3 o'clock in the morning.

Question by the court. Did the Genl, in your opinion, do every thing in his power, to annoy and repel the enemy, and save the country from desolation?

Ans^r. Yes sir, while I was with him, I saw nothing wanting in him.

Quest. by court. Did the Genl at any time discover the least want of personal bravery and firmness in the course of the action, and transactions of the 19th October last?

Ans^r. He did not, but the contrary.

Quest. by court. Did you know that the place where

the enemy crossed the river was a common fording place?

*Ans*ʳ. I did not, nor was it. The bank at the place where they crossed was breast high from the water, and the water was deep.

Quest. Was it very dark on the evening of the action?

*Ans*ʳ. I do not think it was fifteen minutes after the firing commenced, before it was so dark as to render it impossible to distinguish one person from another at a distance of ten paces.

The court adjourned till to-morrow at 7 o'clock.

The court met pursuant to adjournment. Mr. Sampson Dyckman being sworn, says. That he joined General Rensselaer about five miles above Schenectady, at three or four o'clock on the afternoon of the day the Gen¹ marched from Schenectady. That when he came up with the Gen¹ the troops were marching with expedition, and continued so till evening, being then about fourteen or sixteen miles from Schenectady, where they halted till moon rise.

That just as the moon rose, the Gen¹ came to the encampment and ordered the troops to prepare and march immediately, and that in five minutes they moved. That the Gen¹ informed him the enemy were some distance ahead and that he expected his troops would soon fall in with them. That the road over Chucktinunda Hill was very bad, miry and deep, which impeded the march. That they arrived at Fort Hunter at about 12 o'clock and crossed instantly in a scow, on waggons and on horseback, and proceeded in their march without delay. That when the roads were good, the troops marched very fast, but where the roads were bad, they were delayed by the artillery and waggons.

Question by General Rensselaer. Did not you come to me with a request that the troops might not be ordered to march so fast?

Ans^r. I did wait on you, at the instance of Major Schuyler and others, who said the men would not be fit for action, in case they were marched so fast. You then told me, that the enemy were ahead destroying the country, and the men must be marched fast at all events, to come up with them. Many of the men were much fatigued by ten o'clock next morning so as to render it necessary for them to go on horseback and in the waggons.

The court adjourned till 5 o'clock P. M.

The court met pursuant to adjournment.

Major Lewis R. Morris, being sworn, says, That he overtook Genl Rensselaer at Mr H. Glen's at Schenectady, on the 18th October last, at about 12 o'clock and joined him as a volunteer aid-de-camp. That he was there ordered by the Genl to assist Mr Le Roy, his Major of Brigade in getting the troops out of town.

That the troops marched out of town about one and a half miles on the low lands where they were formed and ordered to march into sections to the Woestyne at Mr Van Eps, about nine miles from Schenectady, where they halted to refresh themselves for a very short time, and then marched to Sir Williams old place.[1] That it was then dark, and the troops halted till moon-rise about ten or eleven o'clock. The deponent was then informed that the Gen' and field officers on consultation, tho't it imprudent and dangerous to march over the Chicktinunda Hill in the night till moon rise, and the troops were accordingly halted on the side of the road.

That the deponent thereafter attended the advanced corp under Lt. Col. Pratt[2] and Major McKinster. That about moon rise, the Gen' ordered the troops in motion, and marched to Fort Hunter, and that the troops immediately crossed the river, or Schoharie creek in scows, and while the Gen' was examining two deserters from the enemy. That the troops were halted on the west side of Schoharie creek till the artillery came up, which had gone a different route and joined them in a short time.

That the troops then marched on without delay to Van Eps, where they arrived about four o'clock and halted not more than an hour. That during that halt, letters were written by order of the Gen' to Col° Dubois and Col° Brown, informing them of his approach with

---

[1] Three miles west of the present village of Amsterdam.
[2] David Pratt, appointed lieutenant colonel, Nov. 4th, 1778.

a body of troops, and that these letters were given in charge to a Mr. Wallace.

That soon after the letters were dispatched, the troops were put in motion; that the day then began to dawn. That the roads were very bad and the troops complained of being very much fatigued. That the whole body marched about four or five miles and halted at the ruins of a house, for a few minutes for the purpose of examining a prisoner taken that night. That the deponent then again joined the advance corps and proceeded on to a bridge, where he and Lt. Col. Pratt discovered a party of the enemy on the opposite side of the river. That the advance corps halted till the deponent rode down about a quarter of a mile to the Gen', (who was advancing with the troops), to inform him of the discovery of the enemy. That as that party of the enemy was out of the reach of musket shot, the Gen' ordered up a piece of artillery, whereupon the enemy dispersed. That the whole of the troops moved on to the south side of the river opposite Major Fry's[1] where (as the deponent had understood) the Gen' intended to cross the troops, but that on his arrival there, he found it impossible. That it was then between eight and ten o'clock.

That a firing was then heard, which, from its direction, was supposed to be at Oswegatchie,[2] and

---

[1] Now opposite Canajoharie village.
[2] A settlement a short distance northeast from Stone Arabia, in Palatine.

which afterwards proved to have been Colo Brown's rencounter with the enemy.

That the advanced corps not being incumbered with any waggons or artillery moved on expeditiously. That with the main body were one ammunition waggon and two pieces of artillery, and that to the best of his knowledge, the baggage waggons were in the rear of the whole.

That the main body moved on to a house about a mile below Fort Rensselaer. That it was then between 10 and 1 o'clock. That the troops halted there, and the Genl then rec'^{d} information of Col^o Brown's defeat. That Col^o Dubois and Col^o Harper there waited on the Genl.

That the troops were ordered to refresh themselves, and the Genl gave orders for their crossing the ford as soon as they had refreshed themselves.

That after delivering the orders for that purpose, the Genl went with Colo Dubois to Fort Rensselaer. That the Deponent rec^d orders from the Genl to go and assist Mr. Le Roy in getting the troops over the ford. That he accordingly exerted himself in assisting Mr Le Roy to get the troops over the river.

That the troops refused to ford the river, and waggons were drove into it, to facilitate their passage. That it was about an hour after the troops came to the ford before they began to cross, and that it was between two and three hours from their first arrival before they were all over.

That they crossed this ford in different ways. In some instances the waggons were drove into the river, behind each other, and the troops passed from one to the other by wading on the tongues. That Capt" Driskill came down to the ford, with orders from the Gen¹ to hasten the crossing of the troops, and that Mr. Lansing also came and exerted himself in getting them over the river.

That after they had all crossed, they were marched with dispatch to the Ferry where they joined the levies and Indians. That the General did there take the command of the whole.

That after he had joined, the whole were divided into three columns; the right composed of levies, and the left and centre of militia. That the Oneida Indians marched between the left and centre but sometimes changed their situation.

That the troops marched in this order in pursuit of the enemy for some miles. That the centre and left columns were then subdivided, and continued their march.

That Colo Harper came to the Gen¹ and advised him that an Oneida Indian had discovered the enemy near at hand on the low grounds. That soon thereafter, the deponent discovered them drawn up in order. That the Gen¹ then ordered Mr. Lansing to the right, and the deponent to the left.

That the firing on the enemy from the advance party of the centre then commenced about (200) two hundred yards distance. That about the same time, Colo Cuyler's Regiment of the left column began to fire on the enemy at about four hundred yards distance.

That the Gen¹ desired the Deponent to go to the left and order them to cease firing, and advance towards the enemy. That he thereupon went to the left and communicated the Gen¹ˢ orders, but that it was a considerable time before he could effect it.

That that regiment advanced a little, and inclined towards the river when the deponent left it.

That Colo Rensselaer's Reg^t was advanced towards the enemy in an orchard in front of Klock's house. That after delivering the orders to Colo Cuyler's Reg^t, he returned to the General, whom he found in the centre, with Col° Rensselaer's & Whiting's reg^{ts} which were then in the greatest disorder and confusion, and that the Gen¹ did exert himself to get them in order again.

Question by the Court. At what time did the firing commence?

Ans^r. At about sunset, and continued for about thirty minutes.

Quest. by the Court. Did the general discover any want of personal bravery and firmness, in the action of that day?

Ans^r. He did not.

Quest. by the Court. Was Colo Cuyler's Reg't also in disorder and confusion?

Ans^r. They were.

Quest. by the Court. What was the extreme distance between the front and rear of that regiment?

Ans^r. About two hundred and fifty or three hundred yards.

Quest. by Gen^t Rensselaer. Did not the rear of the left fire at the same time when the front did?

Ans^r. They did.

Quest. by Gen^t Rensselaer. Did you hear the reason assigned for ordering a retreat?

Ans^r. I did. I think the reason was, that the troops were in such confusion that it would be easy for a small party of the enemy to cut them to pieces.

Quest. by the Court. Did the Genl thro' the whole of his march from Schenectady upwards, discover a solicitude to come up with the enemy?

Ans^r. He even appeared anxious to come up with them.

Quest. by the Court. What was Genl Rensselaer's conduct the day after the action?

Ans^r. Colo Dubois with the levies marched in pursuit of the enemy the next morning, and the Genl then ordered some light troops from the regiments of militia who were best able to march, to go as volunteers to overtake Col^o Dubois. That the dep^t went accordingly with about thirty volunteers. That on his way, the General with a party of horse, passed him at the Castle[1] and that the deponent with his party

---

[1] In the present town of Danube, opposite the mouth of East Canada creek.

marched on and scarse came up with the Genl and Col^o Dubois at Fort Herkimer.

That as soon as the main body of militia came up, the whole force marched in pursuit of the enemy about three or four miles above Fort Herkimer at Shoemakers', where they halted for some time. That a difference of opinion then arose on the route the enemy had taken, and on a consultation of the field officers, the whole of the troops returned to Fort Herkimer, where the Govr took the command.

Quest. by Genl Rensselaer. Do you not recollect that I sent out three or four Indians to discover the enemy's track?

Ans^r. I do.

Edward S. Willet, being sworn, says: That on the day of the action of the 19th October last, he was attached to the artillery. That he was at Fort Rensselaer and afterwards with Genl Rensselaer and Colo Dubois, on the bank of the river at the ferry. That he there received orders from the Genl to go down to the place where the militia were crossing, and desire the officers to hurry on the troops as quick as possible, which he did.

Quest. by Genl Rensselaer. Do you not remember that the artillery and ammunition waggons frequently halted on account of the badness of the roads?

Ans^r. I do, and particularly at and above Anthony's Nose, where the ammunition waggon was delayed the horses being very much fatigued.

Lieut. Garret W. Van Schaick,¹ being sworn says: That he was in the field of action on the 19th Oct. last:

That when Col° Cuyler's Regiment, and the other troops were advancing towards the enemy then yet out of the reach of musket shot, Col° Cuyler's reg^t began to fire upon the enemy, and rushed on a few paces, which broke the line or order they were in. That soon after, they were in great disorder and confusion and the deponent saw Genl Rensselaer with them, endeavoring to form them. That the Genl exerted himself greatly on this occasion, but his efforts were fruitless. That the troops were worn down with fatigue occasioned by the long and rapid march and the want of rest the preceding night.

The court adjourned till Tuesday morning.

7 o'clock, *March* 15th, 1780.

The court met pursuant to adjournment and adjourned till the 16th at 6 o'clock P. M.

March 16th the court met.

Col° Samuel Clyde,² being sworn says. That on the day of the action of the 19th October last, he commanded a party of Tryon county militia. That he was at Wolrod's ferry near Fort Rensselaer at the time when Genl Rensselaer with the militia arrived at Adam Countryman's, about a mile below it. That he

---

¹ First lieutenant of Captain Rosebooms's company, March 3,1780.

² Commander of the Canajoharie district regiment; appointed Jan. 25, 1778.

crossed the ferry to the north side with the levies and militia, about one o'clock P. M. by Col° Dubois' orders. That he had orders to halt there till Gen¹ Rensselaer should join him.

That about three or four hours thereafter, the Gen¹ with his militia joined the levies and militia at the ferry, when without the least delay, the whole force marched with the greatest expedition till they came up with the enemy. That the militia commanded by the deponent were attached to the levies under Colo. Dubois on the right.

That the deponent was not informed of the disposition of the other troops, and had no opportunity to observe it, as he marched immediately into the woods on the hill. That the troops marched about four miles, till they had got above Col°. Klock's. That he then heard a firing near Klock's house; but that the right continued their march with design to out flank the enemy. That upon finding that the right had got above the enemy, two or three platoons of levies and militia were detached (by Maj. Benschoten) from the rear, to attack a body of the enemy who were posted about one hundred rods above Klock's. That that detachment fired six or seven platoons when the enemy fled, and the troops returned to their post.

That the right was then ordered to halt, until Col°. Dubois waited on the Gen¹ for orders.

That it was then so dark as to render it difficult to enter into action with safety; as it was hardly possible to distinguish our troops and the enemy from one another. That he then observed a cross fire upon the right, from the low lands, which he supposed to have come from the enemy, but that he was the same evening informed by Col°. Dubois, that it proceeded from our own troops.

That the right remained in that situation for about half an hour. That the enemy could just be discerned and part of them were then heard crossing the river. That the daylight was then in, and the troops received orders to march, and they proceeded towards Klock's house, where they halted a short space of time.

That on hearing the groanings of a man that lay wounded in the field of action, he detached six men to bring him in. That these men with some others, brought in the artillery waggons and artillery which had been deserted by the enemy. That a report of this matter was sent to Gen¹. Reusselaer, two or three hours after dark.

That it was agreed between this deponent and Maj. Benschoten to halt the troops and remain on the ground where they were, and that soon after, Col°. Dubois came to them with orders that they should remain on the ground near Klock's.

That he did not hear of any council of war being held, and a retreat resolved on. That Col° Dubois informed the deponent and Maj. Benschoten, that the Gen¹ would be with them in the morning, and that they were to march in pursuit of the enemy.

That the levies under Col⁰. Dubois, and the militia commanded by the deponent, marched accordingly about an hour after sunrise, and before the Gen¹ came up with them. That he heard the Gen¹ lodged at Fox's about three or four miles below Klock's. That Col⁰. Dubois and the deponent, and their troops marched to Fort Herkimer and arrived there about two o'clock, being about eighteen or twenty miles. That about an hour after, they were joined by the general with a party of horse, and that some time thereafter, Major Morris, with a party of militia came up; and that about two hours after the General's arrival they were joined by a body of militia. That then (about four o'clock), all the troops marched from Fort Herkimer (about six miles), to Shoemaker's.

Gen¹ˢ Question. Do you know the reason of our marching to Shoemaker's?

Ansʳ. The enemy had marched into the woods, and it was supposed they only meant to avoid the little forts which were along the public road, and would come into the road again at Shoemaker's.

Gen¹ˢ Quest. Did you not hear that we were at a loss to know which way the enemy had gone, and do you not recollect that three Indians were sent out by me to discover their track?

A. I did hear that it was doubtful which route the enemy had taken and that the Indians were sent out.

Quest. Did we remain there that night, or did we

return,—and when—and do you know the reason of our return?

Ans. We remained there till near dark, and then returned to Fort Herkimer. I do not know the reason why. I heard the scouts had been out and returned, and that they could not discover that the enemy had gone that way.

Quest. Did not the governor join us at Fort Herkimer?

Ans. He did, some time in that night.

Quest. Had you on the 19th Octr from your situation, any opportunity of seeing the confusion that prevailed on our left and centre?

Ans. I had not.

Quest. Do you think it would have been prudent in me, to have engaged the enemy with the party of levies and militia who were on the north side of the river, at Wolrod's ferry, before the militia who were below came up?

Ans. I do not think it would.

Quest by the Court. Did you on the 19th or 20th October, or at any time before, discover any want of personal bravery and firmness in Genl Rensselaer?

Ans. I never did, before, nor did I at any time on those days.

John Lansing Junr, Esqr. being sworn, says as follows: On the 17th of October last, in the afternoon, I accompanied Genl Rensselaer in quality of Aid-major from Albany to Schenectady. The city of

Albany militia, and some other regiments having previously proceeded on their march to that place. We overtook and passed a number of the militia before we arrived at that place, and Col^o. Van Alstyne's reg^t which had been directed to march by the way of Nestagiuna, not having arrived at Schenectady in the evening, the general sent an express to him, with orders to hasten his march, so as to be at Schenectady at daybreak next morning.

In the mean time, the general having been informed that the enemy were still burning in the lower parts of Schoharie, convened some of the principal inhabitants of Schenectady, and advised with them on the practicability of procuring a number of horses and waggons by the next morning, to convey such militia as could be collected, towards the enemy, with the greatest expedition.

The attempt was made in the course of the night, but a number very inadequate to the service could only be procured. The issuing commissary was the same evening sent for to inform the general of the state of provisions at Schenectady. It appeared from his information, as I was advised by Genl Rensselaer an hour or two after he was sent for, that there was not a sufficiency of provisions of the meat kind to victual the troops for a day, and a very small quantity of bread. Some cattle arriving destined for the garrison of Fort Schuyler, the general ordered some of them to be killed for the use of the militia. Those were to have been ready at daybreak, but the bread which was ordered to be baked, and the cattle directed to be killed, did not get ready till about nine o'clock in the morning, before which orders were issued to march as soon as the provisions should be received.

While we were at Schenectady on the morning of the 18th, General Rensselaer wrote a letter, or directed me to write to Colonel Staats or Veeder (I cannot charge my memory to which), directing him, as nearly as I can recollect, to call upon Major Woolsey, and to take all the force he could collect from the different posts at Schohary, without exposing the forts too much, pursue the enemy, and hang on their rear, avoiding however an engagement, and advising the General from time to time, of the route, numbers, and such other particulars respecting the enemy as he could collect.

I believe it was between nine and ten o'clock before the militia got in march. They marched on the 18th, as far as Sir William Johnson's old place on the Mohawk River, which I think I was informed was sixteen miles above Schenectady. We arrived there after it was dark, and took post on a hill.

A council was called by the General as soon as the troops could be properly disposed of, consisting of a number of field officers and the General suggested to them the necessity of taking measures to procure intelligence of the enemy's route. It was agreed to send out a party to make discoveries, and which was accordingly done. The Tughtenunda[1] Hill being covered with woods, and it being very dark, the council agreed in sentiment, that it would be most advisable to remain on the ground on which we then were, till the moon should begin to appear. We accordingly remained I think till some time before the moon rose, when the march was resumed. We arrived at Fort Hunter (I think) about twelve. The militia were directed to cross the Schoharie creek, which was soon effected in a scow and the waggons.

I went into the fort with the General, who examined a prisoner that had been taken and brought in, and upon coming out we crossed the creek and found most of the militia on the west side. We then marched on, and I do not recollect that we made any halt after leaving the creek, till we got to Van Ep's where we halted, I think about an hour. Here the General directed me to write to Colonels Dubois and Brown, advising them of his situation and his intentions to pursue the enemy closely, and to attack them by break of day. In consequence of these orders, I wrote a letter to Col° Dubois, of which I believe the paper Col° Harper produced to the court is a copy. Another was dispatched to Colonel Brown. The General received the account at Van Eps, by one Wallace, that the enemy were encamped at Anthony's Nose, on both sides of the river, we continued our march to a field

---

[1] Chuctanunda.

at some distance from the east side of the Nose. It was then some time advanced in the day. Here we halted. The ammunition was inspected, and an additional quantity distributed among the troops. Colonel Louis was sent out to reconnoitre Anthony's Nose, which is a very dangerous defile.

Upon his return, and reporting that he had made no discoveries, and after the issues of ammunitions were completed, which might possibly have taken an hour, the militia were ordered on. After proceeding to the west side of the Nose, we discovered a party of about forty of the enemy on the north side of the Mohawk River who were bending their course towards the river. Our advance was then about one quarter of a mile in front of the main body. Captn Driskill of the artillery was with a field piece with the advance guard. I was directed by the Genl to go to the advance guard and order the officer commanding it, to make proper dispositions to intercept the enemy, should they cross a ford, which it was said was in our front, as the general supposed they mistook our troops for those of the enemy. I rode to the advance, and delivered my orders. They halted for some time, and Capt Driskill upon my returning desired me to beg the general to give the enemy's party a shot or two. When I returned, I communicated Driskill's request. Genl Rensselaer observed to me, our business was not so much to frighten the enemy as to fight them, and that a compliance with Driskill's request would only tend to discover to the enemy that we were in force. We continued marching on, without making any general halt, that I recollect, till we arrived at the ford, about a mile to the eastward of Fort Rensselaer. The militia stopped here to refresh themselves not having had time to cook their provisions since their leaving Schenectady, the enemy being then burning from the direction of their fires at Stone Arabia.

Soon after the halt, Gen¹ Rensselaer went to Fort Rensselaer, to which place I followed him and dined. Immediately after dinner, Gen¹ Rensselaer directed me to go down to the militia and order them across the river as soon as possible. When I came down to the place where they had halted, I found that some had already crossed the river on waggons and others were following their example. But they went across very tardily, complaining of being too much harrassed by a forced march and many appeared much dispirited on account of Brown's defeat which was generally known among them.

Imagining that the crossing would be expedited by forming a bridge across the river with our waggons, I suggested it to some of the field officers who agreed with me in sentiment, but the orders given for the execution of this service, were executed with such reluctance, that at least two hours elapsed before the militia had crossed, tho' many of the officers exerted themselves to facilitate their conveyance across the river.

While the militia were crossing, I received two messages from the General, to push them on with all expedition, which was communicated to the field officers on the ground.

In the mean time, an attempt was made to induce them to ford the river, but proved unavailing. As soon as they were crossed, they were marched to the place where the levies had crossed the river, and were formed and counted off in sections. The enemy were then about two miles in advance, burning the buildings as they proceeded.

After we had marched on some distance, the general directed me to write a letter to his Excellency the Governor, advising him that he was near the enemy, and intended to attack as soon as he could overtake them. While I was writing, the disposition of the troops was made for an attack.

Upon my overtaking the General, who was at the head of what I was told was the centre column, I rode with him some minutes, when he observed to me, that the militia on the left, were marching on without observing any order, and directed me to go to them, and order them to march more compactly. I went down and gave the orders to Colonel Cuyler and some other officers. Upon my return to the General, I observed a number of men in advance of the centre, as I afterwards found, and upon my taking the shortest route towards them, I found they were Indians. I enquired of one of them whether he had seen the

General. He happened not to understand me, and while I was endeavoring to make him understand me the Indians began to fire, and received a warm one in return. The first fire, my horse fell with me. By this time, the troops in the low ground had commenced a firing at long shot from the enemy, broke, and some ran. I again made an attempt to mount my horse, but finding that he would not stand fire, I ran down towards the left, one of the militia attending me and leading my horse, till I came to Van Alstyne's regiment which was broke. I assisted in rallying it, which was partly effected. I then went to Colonel Cuyler's and endeavored to assist the officers in rallying that regiment, which was also partly rallied: but part of another regiment (Van Alstyne's I think) firing at Cuyler's they again broke, and could not be rallied.

A similar confusion seemed to prevail in every part of the troops on the left. I did not see General Rensselaer after the firing commenced, till it had somewhat subsided, and from the direction of the fire, it appeared that the enemy's had entirely ceased, when he exerted to rally Cuyler's and other regiments on the left. He observed to me, that the confusion and darkness was such, that it would be imprudent to engage the enemy in the night, and directed me to assist in marching off the troops.

When the firing commenced on our part, the rear of two regiments in the low grounds, were strung along a hundred and fifty or two hundred yards behind the front, and kept up a warm fire, as well as the front, but the direction of the fire seemed to be up in the air.

At the time the engagement began it was dark, and in a few minutes it was quite dark, which I believe was occasioned by the smoke of the buildings which were burnt by the enemy.

Immediately after the firing on the part of the enemy ceased, I heard several exclamations at different times, by the militia on the low grounds, that they were in danger to be cut to pieces and surrounded by the enemy and many of them expressed a great disposition to run off.

In the evening of the action, I suggested to the general, that the troops were without provisions and I recollect he informed me, that he had ordered the provisions to be over early in the morning, but it did not arrive till after sunrise.

In the same evening, the General informed me, that he had given orders to Col°. Dubois, for the marching of the levies in pursuit of the enemy the next morning, by break of day, or before day, (I do not recollect which), and those troops marched accordingly.

As soon as the militia had got their provisions and cooked and eat it, they marched also, I think about an hour after sunrise (but this I cannot ascertain with precision).

On the march, the general desired that a small detachment of men of the different regiments who were best able to go on, should turn out as volunteers, to overtake, and who went on to join Colº. Dubois. If I recollect right, this detachment was made in consequence of intelligence received, that Colº. Dubois was very near the enemy.

The General went on, escorted by a small number of horsemen, to join Colº. Dubois. I followed him, and we arrived at Fort Herkimer about two o'clock. About two hours after, the militia joined us and halted a small space of time.

. Here the General received intelligence, that the enemy had struck off from the public road to avoid the fort, and had taken the route to Shoemaker's.

The General then marched the troops on to near Shoemaker's. It was there become doubtful what route the enemy had taken, and parties of Indians and white men were sent out to discover their track who returned and finally reported that from the observations they could make, the enemy had not gone that way.

When the general found that he had mistaken the enemy's route, he ordered the troops to return to fort Herkimer, with intentions (as was said), to fall in with their track, to the southward of Fort Herkimer. It was just dark, when the troops marched from Shoemaker's towards Fort Herkimer.

The next morning the governor took the command.
Question by the Court. From the whole tenor of

Gen¹ Rensselaer's conduct in his march up the Mohawk River, had you reason to suppose that he was anxious to come up with the enemy?

*Ans*ʳ. He appeared to be very much so, in every part of his conduct.

Quest. by Court. Did you, in or before the action of the 19th October, discover any want of firmness, or personal bravery in the general?

*Ans*ʳ. From what I observed of his conduct, before the action, he appeared to possess himself fully, and in the course of that action, or after it he did not betray the least want of resolution or firmness, as far as fell under my observation.

The court then adjourned till Saturday morning, March 17th, at 7 o'clock.

The court met pursuant to adjournment.

Upon duly considering the proofs and allegations respecting B. Gen¹ Rensselaer's conduct on the incursions of the enemy into Tryon county, in October last: The Court do unanimously report their opinion: That the whole of General Rensselaer's conduct both before and after, as well as in, the action of the 19th of October last, was not only unexceptionable, but such as became a good, active, faithful, prudent and spirited officer, and that the public clamors raised to his prejudice on that account, are without the least foundation.

JACOBUS SWARTWOUT, Presdᵗ

His Excellency, Governor Clinton.

Memorial of the Supervisors of Tryon County.

At a meeting of the supervisors of Tryon county on the 20th day of December, 1780:

The supervisors being convened according to the directions of the several acts for raising men during the war; for raising by tax a sum equal to 150,000 dollars in specie, and for drawing forth the supplies allotted to this state passed in the last setting of the legislature:—and having taken the same into consideration, are obliged to observe, that in the former situation of the county, the quotas allotted to us might have been raised, but that in the present situation, we are persuaded, that as to the two former acts, it is out of the power of the county to comply with them, without distressing us in the highest degree. The latter cannot be complied with, without starving great numbers of people who have been burned out and abandoned their plantations. The poverty and inability of our people are such, that we think that in the present impoverished state of the country, it is unjust and unreasonable to be called upon for such large proportions of men, money and supplies, willing and ready as we always have been in our exertions for the public good, we cannot be understood to censure the legislature for passing the laws, for at the time thereof, we think we might have raised our quotas, but we mean to show that at present we have not that ability.

In order to set the state of the country in a proper point of view, we have with great trouble and labor, got attested returns made of the number of buildings burned, of families moved from their plantations, of persons ran away to the enemy, of the number killed and taken prisoners, and as near as could be, the farms which lie uncultivated by reason of our defenceless situation: — By which it appears, that 700 buildings have been burnt, 354 families have abandoned their plantations and moved from the county, 613 persons have deserted to the enemy, 197 persons have been killed, 121 persons are prisoners with the enemy. The number of uncultivated farms in consequence of incursions by and desertions to the enemy amounts to at least 1,200.

The whole of the county is not included in the above. Returns from Cherry Valley, Newtown-Martin, Springfield, Harpersfield and Old England district, by reason of a total desertion of these settlements could not be got. The inhabitants have some deserted to the enemy, the greater number moved in.

When the above was made up, returns from three companies in Colonel Fisher's regiment had not come in, one of which is nearly burned out.

To make our misery and distress appear clear, it is observable, that in Col° Bellinger's regiment, which comprehends the German Flatts and Kingsland districts, there are not more than forty-four farms cultivated, on which live 139 families, besides the owners, the produce whereof in time of peace would not maintain more than 183 families, so that making allowance for the dangers we are daily exposed to, they have not sufficient by a great deal for their subsistence. Eighty-eight families have moved lower down.

That in Col° Klock's regiment, comprehending Palatine district, the greater part of the buildings are destroyed with the grain, one full third of the farms lie uncultivated, and not above 50 farmers left, who have any grain to spare: added to the large number of refugees from the upper Canajohary districts makes it evident beyond a doubt that this district has not bread till the ensuing harvest.

The greater half of Canajohary is destroyed; some parts so long ago as 1778, which since have not been tilled; some part last summer. The devastation and property of the inhabitants and refugees in this district are such, that the grain in it will be barely sufficient for the subsistence of those who remain in it.

Caughnawaga district in Col° Fisher's regiment, is equally distressed with the two last having a large number of disaffected people on its back parts, who are a continual terror to the well affected, who in order to aid the country, raise no more than a sufficiency for themselves, with the double destruction of the ablest part of the district has undergone the part remaining being poor in general, added to a total destruction of a great part of the district shew a melancholy truth that all the grain remaining therein, will not keep the inhabitants and refugees resident, till they can have the benefit of a new crop.

The Mohawk District in Col° Fisher's Regiment, has suffered the least by the enemy and is not so much burthened with refugees as the others,—has some grain to spare, but when the other parts of the country are supplied, what they fall short out of the superfluities of the Mohocks, we apprehend that the quantity remaining will not be great.

The causes of our distress arise chiefly from the following.

The situation of the country make it an entire frontier, exposed to the inroads of the enemy from the north, west and south. The frequent irruptions and many murders committed by the enemy, the constant dread of a repetition thereof, have induced the people to build numbers of small picketed forts, in which they are cooped up from spring to fall, the militia being at half of their time on duty. The difficulty if not impossibility in these cases to work our lands. The work that is done, is performed by halfs only, and under continual fear of the tomahawk and scalping knife. The farms cultivated, are only those which lie near the picquets. The great and heavy losses sustained by us in lives, prisoners, desertions to the enemy, and [in] property, have occasioned the removal from the country of a very large number of families most of them our wealthiest people, and to dishearten those who remain, numbers more are now preparing to follow those already gone.

The people think, that what remains of this once flourishing county will be destroyed the ensuing summer. The nature of the war in these parts is such, that a small force may do it.

Having literally sacrificed our lives and fortunes, in defence of the Liberties of America, the supervisors are sorry to hold up the language of despondence, but the justice we owe to ourselves our constituents and our country, the apprehensions we entertain that the peculiar circumstances of this county, and the great distresses of the people have never been fully made known by those whose duty it was, render it indispensible. The necessity of the case obliges us to do it, in the plain language of truth and without exaggeration.

We cannot help representing as grievances, that upwards of one hundred tory women with destitute families are remaining in Caughnawaga district. The collection of the rents from the tenants of Sir John Johnson and Col⁰ Butler in the same district, due since the Declaration of Independence, at this time fall exceeding hard on that district, as thereby that grain is taken away, which is necessary for their consumption.

As the taking away cattle, at the point of the bayonet might have been necessary for the subsistence of troops, we do not complain of it, but the refusal of proper vouchers by those who executed that business, is a grievance we cannot overlook. The large numbers of stock drove off by the enemy, at different times, makes the hardship of having our cattle seized the greater.

The consequences of the depreciation of the paper currency is, that we can obtain neither the necessaries nor conveniences of life but by barter for grain.

Money we have none, as the supplies furnished the public for upwards of a year past, are not yet paid.

The depreciation it is confessed, has arisen from several causes. Whatever cause it is ascribed to, we feel ourselves entirely free of it, as we can make it appear, that until the last spring, the prices were always lower with us than below, and we seldom if ever received the current price below for our grain here.

The reasons that we have not raised every tax demanded of us by law, are, as to one tax, a disagreement between the supervisors and assessors in assessing the estate real and personal, and as to the others, the want of money, the destitution of the country, and the consequent misery and distress of its inhabitants, arising from the causes, and in the manner above related.

It is ordered that a fair copy of the above be made and transmitted to his Excellency the Governor, and that the clerk of this board sign the same.

Signed by order of the Supervisors.

Isaac Paris, Clerk.

Report of Losses in the Territory of the Tryon County Brigade, since the beginning of the War. Made December 1, 1780.

Regiments, &c.	Number of persons present.	Run away.	Houses burnt.	Barns burnt.	Mills burnt.	Persons killed.	Persons taken prisoners.	Families moved.	Carts burnt.	Saw mills burnt.
Col. Bellinger's Reg't	139	25	131	112	5	50	46	52		
" Klock's	354	35	154			48	27	97	1	
" Fisher's	600	470	105		5	23	13	83		2
Capt. Cloyt's	293	73	69	58	1	71	38	86	1	
" Huber's Comp		10	64			5	10	36		2
Total	1,386	613	523	170	11	197	134	354	2	4

Persons who have gone to the enemy:

Adam Helmer & son, Peter Doring, William Cox, Jacob Didrich, Robert Smicht and Rudolph Schoemarker.

Capt. Herter reported 36 houses, 29 barns and 2 mills as burned, 6 males and 2 females killed, 3 males taken prisoners, and 24 males and 28 females who had moved out of the district since the commencement of the war.

Capt. Staring reported 38 houses 34 barns and 3 mills burnt, 26 males and 5 females killed; 16 males and 3 females taken; and 3 males and 33 females moved out since beginning of the war.

Capt Fred Frank in the like period reported 64 houses 55 barns and 3 mills burned, 36 males and 10 females killed, 37 males and 11 females taken, and 11 males and 44 females moved out of the district.

INDEX.

Alarms, 31, 33, 40.
Albany, Address of Common Council, of, 137; County, 24; Gov. Clinton goes to, 96; Militia, 36, 198; Quota, 90; troops for, 101.
Allen, Captain, 77.
Allen, Ebenezer, 57.
Allen, Ethan, jealousy of, 39, 83, 145.
Allen, Major, 29.
Ambuscade near Oneida Lake, 130; of Col. Brown, 15.
Amsterdam, 179, 187.
Andrustown, 22, 119.
Anthony's Nose, 28, 54, 173, 193, 201, 202.
Arnold, Col. Brown's quarrel with, 157.
Arnold's treason, allusion to, 63, 64, 98, 157, 158.
Articles of Confederation, 41; of capitulation of Fort George, 92.
Assessment of supplies, 83.
Atoiatonharonkwen, 173.

Backus, John, 787.
Ballston, 18, 124, 131, 132, 134, 141, 144; enemy at, 45, 90, 105.
Barrett, Ensign, 44, 92.
Batchellor, Zephaniah, 84.
Bateaux guarded, 33.
Beautiful Elm in Panton, 128.
Becker, John, 48.
Belding, Capt., 97.
Belding, Col., 98.
Bell, George Henry, 118, 119.
Bellinger, Col. Peter, letter of, 65; letter to, from Gov. Clinton, 126; Col., Regiment of, 210, 215.

Benschoten, Major, 170, 189, 195, 196.
Benson, Col., 144.
Benson, Robert, 114.
Bethlehem, N. Y., 113.
Biographical notices: Bellinger, Peter, 65; Brown, Col. John, 57; Cantine, John, 164; Carleton, Chris., 108; Chipman, Capt. John, 100; Cook, Col. Louis, 173; Drake, Joshua, 130; Dubois, Lewis, 119, 165; Duncan, Richard; Gordon, James, 45; Gros, Rev. Johan Daniel, 87; Harper, John, 165; Harper, William, 171; Hughes, Peter, 146; Jansen, Johannis, 70; Lansing, John, Jr., 165; Lush, Stephen, 91; McCracken, Joseph, 129; McKinstry, John, 174; Murphy, Timothy, 52; Patterson, Eleazer, 78; Schuyler, Stephen, 9, 115; Sherwood, Adriel, 43; Snyder, Johannis, 113; Staats, Barent J., 113; Swartwout, Jacobus, 104; Ten Broeck, Abraham, 113; Thomas. Thomas, 164; Van Buntschoten, Elias, 170; Van Rensselaer, Robert, 104; Van Schaick, Col., 9, 67; Van Veghten, Hendrick, 176; Van Woert, Lewis, 143; Veeder, Volkert, 49; Vrooman, Walter, 130; Webster, Allen, 111; Weissenfels, Frederick H., 147; Wempel, Abraham, 131; Woolsey, Melancton L., 48, 51; Yates, Christopher P., 20.
Bleecker, John, 80, 81.
Bloody Pond, 122, 123.
Board of War, 23.

218   INDEX.

Bogart, Capt., 48.
Boston, Convention at, 75.
Bradnor, Lieut., 84.
Brant, Joseph, 17, 19, 26, 30, 33, 34, 42, 47, 55, 68, 76, 86, 89, 93, 96, 106, 154, 174.
Brattleborough. 78.
British Agents, influence of, 31.
Brown, Henry, 58.
Brown, Col. John, 56, 57, 77, 116, 139, 155, 166, 167, 173, 180, 187, 189, 201, 203.
Bryon, Matthew, 66.
Buck Island, 62.
Buffalo, 173.
Bulwagga Bay, 28, 45, 128, 134.
Burgoyne's Invasion, 22, 57, 148.
Butler, Col. John, 17, 42, 47, 76, 89, 93, 96, 106, 154; events due to, 213.
Butler's Regiment, 27.
Butterfield, Benj., 78.

Cadaughrity, 171.
Cadorotty, 171.
Cambridge, N. Y., 142.
Canada, expedition from, expected, 40.
Canajoharie, 20, 26, 34, 58, 85, 88, 115, 125, 138, 139, 188, 194; destroyed, 34, 211, 213; casualties at, 37.
Canaghsioraga, 137.
Canashraga, 130.
Caneseraga, 130.
Cannon, enemy supplied with, 42.
Cautine, Col. John, 164.
Capitulation of Fort George, 32.
Carleton, Major Christopher, 43, 44, 89, 93, 99, 108, 122, 124, 133, 134, 135.
Carleton Island, 120.
Carleton, vessel, 99.
Castle, 192.
Castleton, 143.
Casualties in Tryon county, table of, 215.
Cattle, press warrant for, 120.
Caughnawaga, 55, 123, 173.
Cayuga, N. Y., 146.
Cedars, 173.
Chambly, Col. Brown at, 57.
Charleston, 32.

Charlotte county, 21, 24, 29, 132; quotas, 90.
Cherry Valley, 17, 26.
Chin, Mr., 144.
Chipman, Capt. John, 44, 92, 93, 100, 115.
Chittenden, Gov., letter of, to Gov. Clinton, 111.
Chucktinunda creek, 179.
Chucktinunda hill, 180, 185, 187.
Church burned at Stone Arabia, 116.
Church, Timothy, 78.
Cinge, Adam, 87.
Clapp, Daniel, 154.
Clark, Major, 69.
Claverack, 94, 105.
Clinton, Gov. DeWitt, 88.
Clinton, Gov. George, 29, 38, 53, 54, 61, 204; letters to, from Col. Van Schaick, 67, 74; Lt. Col. Johannis Jansen, 69, 71; Col. J. Newkirk, 73; Gen. R. Van Rensselaer, 76, 94, 103, 115, 117; Col. E. Patterson, 77; citizens of Tryon county, 83; Stephen Lush, 89; Gen. W. Heath, 101; Col. B. L. Staats, 106; Gov. T. Chittenden, 111; Isaac Stoutenburgh, 112; Gen. Ten Broeck, 113, 114, 142, 150; Col. Lewis Du Bois, 119; Gen. Schuyler, 123, 140; Col. A. Webster; Gen. Washington, 159; letters of, to Col. Jansen, 69; Col. Newkirk, 70; Col. Pawling, 72; Gen. Washington, 74, 97, 151, 157; citizens of Cumberland county, 78; Col. G. Van Schaick, 81; Gen. P. Schuyler, 82, 105, 125; Col. Klock, 87, 126; Gen. Van Rensselaer, 95; Gen. Greene, 96; Col. Bellinger, 126; Ebenezer Russell, 132; James Duane, 143; Gen. Heath, 147; address of mayor and council of Albany; 137; reply of, 139.
Clinton, Sir Henry, 32.
Clinton, General James, to command at Albany, 42, 82, 161.
Clinton Co., 48.

INDEX. 219

Clothing, want of, 156; supplied, 80, 81.
Clothing agent, 80.
Cloyt, Capt., 215.
Clyde, Col. Samuel, testimony of, 194.
Columbia College, 88.
Conawaga destroyed, 85.
Connecticut, delegates from, 75.
Connecticut Valley, expedition to, 46, 139.
Connestigone, 178.
Convention of States at Boston, 75.
Cook, Col. Louis, 173, 202.
Coppernoll, Nicholas, 87.
Cornplanter, anecdote of, 35.
Cornwallis, 163.
Countryman, Adam, 87, 174, 194.
Court of Inquiry, proceedings of, 164; decision of, 208.
Cox, William, 215.
Crown Point, 27, 45, 116, 155.
Cruelty of Indians, alleged, 44.
Cumberland County, 21, 24, 38, 78.
Cushing, Thomas, 75.
Cuyler, Mr., 116.
Cuyler, Col., 60, 142, 176, 181, 191, 204, 205.

Danae, Ship, 133.
Decision of Court of Inquiry, 208.
Depreciation of currency, 38, 214.
Deserter, 118.
DeWitt, Major, 72, 73.
Deygert, Peter, 8., 84, 87.
Didrich, Jacob, 215.
Dillenbeck, John, 59.
Disaffected families, 84.
Doring, Peter, 215.
Drake, Joshua, 130.
Drake, Col. Samuel, letter to, from Capt. Lawrence, 129.
Driskill, Joseph, 121, 180, 181, 190, 202.
Duane, James, letter to, from Gov. Clinton, 143.
Duane, Mrs., 146.
Dubois, Col. Lewis, 60, 116, 119, 152, 166, 167, 166, 168, 169, 170, 187, 189, 192, 193, 195, 196, 197, 201, 207; Lewis, letter of, to Gen. Van Rensselaer, 118; Gov. Clinton, 119.

Drew, Mr., 157.
Duncan, Capt. Richard, 55.
Dutchess County, 24; quotas, 90.
Dyckman, Sampson, letter of, to Gov. Clinton, 117; testimony of, 185.

East Canada Creek, 142.
Elliott's, 172.
Epitaph of Timothy Murphy, 52.
Escort of provisions, 156.

Faling, John A., 59.
Fall hill, 118, 119.
Federal government, early movement toward, 75.
Feeck, John, 47.
Ferguson, Col., 163.
Ferry, 190.
Fisher, Col., regiment of, 210, 211, 212, 215.
Fishkill, 154, 164.
Florida, N. Y., 172.
Flour, press warrant for, 120.
Floyd, Mr., 146.
Folliot, Geo., 148.
Fonda, Adam, 100.
Fonda, Jellis, 32, 87.
Fonda village, 55.
Foord, Capt., 48.
Ford where the enemy crossed, 185.
Fording of river, 189, 190, 203, 204.
Fort Ann, 24, 43, 57, 89, 93, 96, 98, 99, 106, 122, 133, 136, 155.
Fort Carleton, 62.
Fort Dayton, 23, 85, 127.
Fort Edward, 23, 24, 44, 93, 96, 99, 110, 124, 128, 141.
Fort George, 89, 92, 95, 96, 100, 106, 122, 133, 136, 155.
Fort Herkimer, 23, 61, 62, 76, 119, 127, 147, 148, 156, 193, 197, 198, 207.
Fort Hunter, 24, 54, 104, 107, 116, 144, 171, 172, 177, 179, 180, 185, 187, 201.
Fortifications, location of, 22.
Fort at Johnstown, 28.
Fort Keyser, 57, 59.

220 INDEX.

Fort Niagara, 17, 19.
Fort Paris. 26, 32, 56, 57, 59.
Fort Plain, 23, 76, 116, 166, 168, 173.
Fort Plank, 23, 35, 76.
Fort Rensselaer, 60, 76, 131, 144, 167, 168, 173, 180, 181, 184, 189, 194, 203.
Fort Schuyler, 23, 30, 33, 36, 38, 42, 53, 62, 68, 72, 74, 75, 77, 80, 94, 98, 118, 129, 144, 146, 148, 150, 160, 161, 199.
Fort Stanwix, rumor of capture, 81.
Fort Philip, 152.
Fox's mills, 154, 181, 184.
Frank, Fred., 215.
Fry, Major, 188.
Fultonville, N. Y., 166, 172.

Gage's hill, 122.
Galway, 131.
Gansevoort, Col. Peter, 44, 101, 109, 125, 132, 140, 147, 155, 159.
Gardinier's Flatts, 172.
Garlock, John Christian, 116.
Garoga creek, 32, 152.
Garrisons of frontier post, 127.
Garrison duty, irksomeness of, 30.
Gates, General. 57.
Gebhard, John, Jr., 53.
Germain, Lord, 63, 133.
German Flatts, 21, 36, 65, 67, 118, 119, 140, 210.
Germantown, 66.
Gillet, Mr., 101.
Glen, Henry, 102, 103, 107, 120, 177, 186.
Glen, H., letter to, from Col. Veeder, 102.
Glen, town of, 173.
Goodman, Dommas, 87.
Granville, 142.
Green, Gen., 97, 101; letter to, from Gov. Clinton, 96.
Grog Bay, 128.
Gros, Johan Daniel, 87.
Gordon, James, 45, 46.
Guilderland, 130.

Haldimand, Governor, 63, 64, 133.

Half Moon Point, 23.
Hall's Poughkeepsie Journal, 95.
Hanover, N. H., 82.
Hanson, Peter, 100.
Harper, Capt. Alexander, 19.
Harper, Col. John, 29, 166, 175, 189, 190, 201; testimony of, 165.
Harper, William, 171.
Harpersfield, 19, 22, 165, 210.
Harris, William, 78.
Harrison, N. Y., 164.
Harvesting protected, 36, 85.
Haughton, Major, 46, 134.
Hay, Col. Uduy, 113, 117, 141.
Heath, General, 83, 150; letter to Gov. Clinton, 101; letter to, from Gov. Clinton, 147.
Hebron, N. Y., 111.
Hellebergh, 131.
Helmer, Adam, 215.
Henderson, Capt., 154.
Hendrick, Leonard, 78.
Herter, Capt., 215.
Herkimer, 23.
Herkimer, Gen. Nicholas, 118.
Hessians, 47.
Hinsdale, Vt., 78.
How, Artemas, 78.
Huber, Capt., 215.
Hughes, Major, 23, 42, 62, 89, 146, 156.

Jansen, Lt. Col. Johannis, 40, 70, 73, 74.
Jansen, Lt. Col. Johannis, letters of, 69, 71; letters to, 69, 71.
Johnson, Sir John, 26, 27, 42, 47, 48, 50, 51, 55, 57, 58, 62, 63, 76, 89, 90, 93, 106, 118, 121, 134, 135, 147, 154, 166, 172, 180; rents due to, 213.
Johnson, Sir William, 55, 179.
Johnson, Sir William, place of, 200.
Johnston, William, 93.
Johnstown, 18, 21, 23, 26, 28, 35, 122, 154; memorial from, 83; Carleton said to be at, 108.

Kaselman, John, 87.
Katskill, 107.
Keator's Rift, 55.

INDEX. 221

Kelman, George, 87.
Keyser, Capt. John, 18.
Killed and wounded, 135, 136.
Kingsbury burnt, 43.
Kingsland district, 65, 210.
Kingston, 97.
Kirkman, James, 93.
Klock, Col. Jacob I., 26, 87, 91.
Klock, Col., letter to, from Gov. Clinton, 87, 126.
Klock, Col., regiment of, 211, 215.
Klock's, field battle of, 60.
Klock's place, 60, 182.
Klock's house, 191, 195, 196, 197.
Knowlton, Mr., 79, 143.

LaFayette, Marquis, 108.
L'Hommedieu, Ezra, 146.
Lairs, Henrick, 87.
Lairs, William, 87.
Lake Champlain, 22, 27, 29, 96, 100, 134, 42, 43, 76.
Lake George, 24, 29, 30, 45, 57, 62, 93, 109.
Lansing, Capt., 48.
Lansing, John, Jr., 151, 165, 166, 190; letter of, to Gov. Clinton, 107; testimony of, 198.
Laurence, Capt. J., Jr., letter of, to Col. S. Drake, 129.
Legislature convened, 40.
LeRoy, Mr., 186, 189.
Levies for defense of frontiers, 25.
Leyp, Adam, 87.
Lincoln, Gen., 57.
Little Falls, 18.
Livingston, Col., 44, 91, 97, 110, 115, 123, 189.
Livingston, Col. Henry, Jr., 117; letter to, from, Capt. Sherwood, 99.
Livingston, Peter, R., 117.
Livingston, Robert, 146.
Livingston, Gov. Wm., 81.
Livingston, N. Y., 74.
Losses of Tryon Co., table of, 215.
Loudon's Packet, article from, 121.
Louis, Col., 202.
Lowville, N. Y., 58.
Luch, Stephen, 91, 97; letter from, to Gov. Clinton, 89.

McAlpin's Regt., 136.
McCracken, Major Joseph, 129.
McCrea, Colonel, 27.
McCrea, Dr. Stephen, 114.
McDonald, Donald, incursion of, 37, 65.
McDonald, a refugee, 45.
McDougall, Gen. Alexander, 146.
McFarlan, Mr., 141.
Machin, Thomas, 157.
McKinstry, Major John, 173, 174, 182, 187.
Malcom, Col. William, 36, 72, 73, 74, 89, 90, 91, 94, 97, 98, 129, 157; letter of, to Gen. Van Rensselaer, 93.
Massachusetts, Delegates from, 75.
Mayfield, 29.
Memacatinge, 71.
Memorial of citizens of Shenectady, 131; of supervisors of Tryon County, 209.
Miami, battle of, 130.
Middleburgh, 21, 47, 48.
Militia, organization of, 24; for guarding forts, 25, 30; rallied in pursuit, 29; sent up Mohawk Valley, 36; might be called out, 41; called out, 43.
Milford, N. Y., 171.
Mills, Abraham, 141.
Minisink, 19, 73.
Mohawk District, 212.
Mohawk Indians, 134.
Monmouth, 148.
Montreal, 26.
Monument to Col. Brown, 58.
Morris, Lewis R., 186, 197.
Mortars, 42, 89, 157.
Mount Defiance, 57.
Mount Independence, 57, 128.
Muller, Capt., 48.
Munro, Major John, 45, 46.
Murphy, Timothy, 51, 52.

Nash, Aaron, 79.
Navigation of Mohawk, 38.
Neponeck, 73.
Nestigiuna, 199.
Nestigona, 178, 179.
New City, 23.
New Hampshire, delegates from, 75.

New Hampshire Grants, 29, 39, 79, 98, 110, 144, 145.
Newkirk, Col., letter to Gov. Clinton, 73.
Newkirk, Jacob, 70, 74.
Newkirk, letter to, from Gov. Clinton, 73; letter of Gov. Clinton, to, 70.
Newport, French at, 75.
Newtown, Battle of, 148.
Newtown-Martin, 22, 210.
Niagara, 31, 42, 86, 89, 134, 135.
Niskayuna, 178.
Niven's Kill, 70.
Norman's Kill, settlements attacked, 35.
Nose (See Anthony's Nose).

O'Bail, 35.
Ocquago, scout to, 77.
Old-England District abandoned, 210.
Old Farms, 172.
Oneida, 153, 154; enemy at, 33, 89, 93; expedition by way of, 42.
Oneida Castle, 23.
Oneida Indians, 152, 190, 194, 204; jealousy of, 18; faithful, 31; removed to Shenectady, 32, 141.
Oneida Lake, expedition by way of, 47.
Oneida settlements, rumored destruction of, 32.
Orange County, 24; quotas, 90.
Ordnance captured from enemy, 121.
Oriskany, battle of, 118.
Oswegatchie, 188.
Oswego, 62, 135.

Palatine, 20, 28, 32, 116, 188.
Palatine Bridge, 56.
Panton, 128.
Paris, Isaac, 33, 214.
Patterson, Col. Eleazer, 71, 78; Letter of, to Gov. Clinton, 77.
Pawling, Col. Levi, 164.
Pawling, Col. Albert, 25, 70, 71, 72; letter to, from Gov. Clinton, 72.
Peasley, 131.

Pellinger, Col., 67.
Petition of citizens of Tryon Co., 85.
Phillips, Major, 73.
Pittsfield, Mass., 57.
Plattsburgh, 48.
Poole, Capt., 48.
Poughkeepsie, 40, 90, 96, 97, 105.
Prackness, 159.
Pratt, Lt. Col. David, 187, 188.
Prisoners, 17, 19, 154.
Provisions, scarce, 90, 92, 94, 98, 102, 117, 206; forwarded, 112.
Putnam's Point, 128, 145.

Quebec, 133.
Queensbury burnt, 44.
Quotas, 99, 162; provided for, 158.

Ray, Mr, 143.
Rayments Mills, 128.
Recruiting for army, 41.
Reinlistment of troops, 25.
Reimensnyder's Bush, 18.
Rensselaer, Gen. See Van Rensselaer.
Rents due to Johnson and Butler, 213.
Rescue from torture, 174.
Reward offered for a spy, 109.
Ries, Rev. John Frederick, 116.
Rivington's Gazette, quotation from, 91.
Roof, Rev. Gerrit L., 58.
Roof, N. Y., 28.
Roseboom, Capt., 194.
Rosendal, 179.
Rosie, John, 178.
Russell, Ebenezer, letter to, from Gov. Clinton, 132.

Sacondaga, 151; Block House, 18.
St. John, 30, 49, 122.
St. Johnsville, 60, 133.
St. Regis, 173.
Safford, Col., 122.
Salem, N. Y., 127, 192.
Saratoga, 23, 70, 109, 114, 115, 123.

INDEX.

Scarcity, complaints of, 211, 212, 261.
Schenectady, 23, 27, 106, 107, 110, 140, 144, 148, 151, 155, 171, 172, 177, 185, 186, 187, 192, 199, 200; troops rallied at, 29; Indians at, 32; expedition intended for, 45; troops arrive at, 53; meeting of citizens of, 54; memorial of, 131.
Schoharie, 23, 109, 127, 144, 151, 157, 177, 200; forts described, 24, 47; troops at, 27; attacked, 19, 47, 49, 102, 105; fires seen at Schenectady, 53.
Schoharie Court House, 49.
Schoharie Kill, 151.
Schoonhoven, Colonel, 27.
Schuyler, Gen. Philip, 82, 105, 109, 114, 123, 145, 165; ordered in a certain case to arrest Allen, 39; notifies appearance of enemy, 42; letter to, from Gov. Clinton, 82, 105, 125; letter of, to Gov. Clinton, 123, 140.
Schuyler, Col. Philip P., 107, 113.
Schuyler, Col. Stephen I., 106, 115.
Schuyler, Major, 186.
Schuyler's Regt., 105, 106.
Scomondo, 31.
Scotch tories, 21.
Scott, George G., 45.
Scott, Gen. John Morin, 146.
Seger, Henry, 78.
Settlements, extent of, in 1780, 21; broken up, 27.
Shawangunk, 40, 69, 71.
Shell, John Christian, 37, 65.
Sherwood, Capt. Adiel, 43, 89, 93, 99, 101, 122, 123; letter of, to Col. H. Livingston, 99.
Sherwood, Mrs., 101.
Shoemaker, Rudolph, 215.
Shoemaker's, 197, 207.
Shoemaker's Land, 120.
Sidney's Mills, 103, 106, 107.
Simms, J. R., 53, 76.
Skeenesborough, 18, 21, 23, 24, 26, 57, 128, 143, 150.
Sloansville, 103.
Smicht, Robert, 215.
Smith, John, 23.
Smith, Joshua H., 157.

Smith, Seth, 78.
Smith, Mr., 79.
Smyth, Dr. George, 100.
Snell, John, 87.
Snyder, Jacob, 141.
Snyder, Col. Johannis, 113.
South Bay, 43.
Southern Campaign, 163.
Sprakers, 55.
Springfield, 22, 210.
Spy at Johnstown, 101.
Staats, Col. B. I., 113, 200; letter of, to Gov. Clinton, 106.
Staring, Capt., 215.
Stone Arabia, 27, 32, 33, 42, 56, 57, 58, 59, 89, 94, 115, 135, 136, 144, 173, 188, 203.
Stone Arabia Patent, 116.
Stone Ridge, 173.
Stone, William L., 26.
Stoutenburgh, Isaac, letter of, to Gov. Clinton, 112.
Sullivan, General, 17, 148.
Supervisors of Tryon Co., memorial of, 209.
Supplies for army, 160, 161.
Susquehannah 21, 47, 65, 154.
Swartwout, Gen. Jacobus, 164, 208.

Taxes in kind, 38, 41, 83, 90.
Ten Broeck, Gen. Abraham, 18, 27, 42, 82, 90, 92, 93, 105, 106, 113, 131, 147, 155, 159; letter of, to Gov. Clinton, 113, 114, 142, 150.
Ten Broeck, Dirck, 113.
Ten Eyck, Lt. Abraham, 80.
Thomas, Col., 164.
Ticonderoga, 57, 116, 124.
Tioga routes, party by way of, 47.
Tories, 21, 26, 29, 125, 141.
Trail of enemy lost, 193, 197, 207.
Treachery of Vermont people suspected, 39.
Treasure of Sir John Johnson, 29.
Treat, Dr. Malachi, 114.
Trenton, N. Y., 48.
Tribe's Hill, 28.
Tryon County, 24; troops sent to, 27; petition from, 42, 85; letter of citizens of, to Gov. Clinton, 83;

Tryon County; quota, 90; brigade, 91; memorial of supervisors, 209; table of losses in, 215.
Tughtenunda Hill, 201.
Tuscarora Indians, 31.

Ulster County, 24; quotas, 90.
Unadilla, scout to, 77.

Van Alstyne, Col., 178.
Van Alstyne, Cornelius, 174.
Van Alstyne's Regt., 205.
Van Bergen, Col. Anthony, 113.
Van Bunschoten, Major Elias, 130, 170.
Van Dresen, James, 44, 124.
Van Eps, 165, 173, 187, 201.
Van Ess, Col., 174.
Vanetta, Samuel, 87.
Van Rensselaer, Henry K., 25.
Van Horne, Rev. Abraham, 58.
Van Rensselaer, Jacob Rutsen, 105.
Van Rensselaer, Gen. Robert, 32, 33, 36, 42, 51, 53 to 56, 59 to 61, 82, 92, 94, 95, 104, 107, 109, 130, 138, 152, 159, 167 to 186, 191, 194 to 205, 208; letter to, from Col. Malcom, 93; Gov. Clinton, 76, 95; Col. Louis Dubois, 118; letter of, to Gov. Clinton, 94, 103, 115, 117; Gen. Court of Inquiry on, 164; notice of, 104.
Van Rensselaer, Stephen, 113.
Van Schaick, Col. G., 25, 27, 29, 30, 81, 97, 102; letter of, to Gov. Clinton, 67, 79, 81.
Van Schaick, Lt. G. W., testimony of, 194.
Van Veghten, Adjutant, 176.
Van Woert, Col., 27, 142, 143, 150; letter of, to Gen. Ten Broeck, 142.
Veeder, Lt. Col. Volkert, 49, 53, 104, 177; letter of, to H. Glen, 102.
Vermont affairs, 38, 39, 77, 78, 145.
Virginia, 163.
Vrooman, Capt. Walter, 65, 130.
Vrooman, Colonel, 29, 127, 142, 153.

Vrooman's Land, 47.

Wallace, William, 188, 201.
Walrath, John, 116, 168.
Warrant for imprisonment, 120.
Warriner, Samuel, 78.
Warner, Colonel, 29, 122.
Warner's Regiment, 122.
Warren, Sir Peter, 172.
Warren, N. Y. 119.
Warrensbush, 172.
Washington, Gen., 30, 36, 39, 79, 96, 98, 102, 105, 106, 108, 145; letter to, from Gov. Clinton, 74, 97; letter of, to Gov. Clinton, 151, 157, 159.
Watson, Capt. James, 67.
Webster, Col. Alexander, 111, 141, 142; letter of, to Gov. Clinton, 128.
Weissenfels, Col., 140, 147, 148, 149, 155, 160.
Wemple, Col. Abraham, 120, 131, 142.
West Canada Creek, 23.
Westchester County, 24; quotas, 90.
West Point, 63, 64, 96, 160.
Wheelock, Rev. Mr., 82.
Whiting, Col., 82.
White Creek, 110, 128, 140, 143; enemy near, 105, 124.
Whitehall, 21.
White Plains, 148.
Whiting, Colonel, 60, 169, 182, 191.
Williams, Col. John, 111.
Williger, 174.
Willow Basin, 54.
Windsor, N. Y., 77.
Woestyne, 187.
Wolrod's ferry, 175, 194, 198.
Wood, Sergeant Wm., 172.
Woodbridge, Col., 157.
Woodward, Solomon, 19.
Woolsey, Major Melancton L., 48, 51, 104, 109, 200.
Wyoming, 17.

Yale, Major, 174.
Yates, Col. Christopher P., 20, 27.

Zielley, Capt. John, 59, 87.

www.ingramcontent.com/pod-product-compliance
Lightning Source LLC
Chambersburg PA
CBHW022015220426
43663CB00007B/1083